AGING AND SOCIETY

SAGE FOCUS EDITIONS

AGING and SOCIETY

Current Research and
Policy Perspectives

Edited by
Edgar F. Borgatta and
Neil G. McCluskey

SAGE PUBLICATIONS   Beverly Hills   London

For information address:

SAGE Publications, Inc.
275 South Beverly Drive
Beverly Hills, California 90212

SAGE Publications Ltd
28 Banner Street
London EC1Y 8QE, England

Printed in the United States of America

Library of Congress Cataloging in Publication Data
Main entry under title:

Aging and society.

(Sage focus editions)
Bibliography: p.
1. Gerontology—United States—Addresses, essays,
lectures. I. Borgatta, Edgar F., 1924
II. McCluskey, Neil Gerard.
HQ1064.U5A6336   301.43'5'0973   79-25727
ISBN 0-8039-1181-5
ISBN 0-8039-1182-3 pbk.

FIRST PRINTING

CONTENTS

INTRODUCTION

RESEARCH ON AGING
IN PERSPECTIVE

Neil G. McCluskey and Edgar F Borgatta

There is a continuing debate as to whether gerontology is a distinct academic discipline, an applied social science, or a hybrid creature of several parent disciplines. Irregardless, after at least three decades of struggling into being but failing to create a notable body of theory, gerontology has at least been endowed by federal budgetary recognition. As a very junior science, it may still have to prove itself before its elders and, more important, if gerontologists want to validate the claim that aging should be a primary area for research, they must make certain that their own house is in order. Perhaps as much as anything else, this thought occasioned the present volume.

The American people are waking to a demographic phenomenon: The numbers and proportion of men and women past 60 have increased to a level unknown before. Social problems and issues now must be studied in a radically altered context, and social policies and planning must be based on new empirical data.

The nation's age composition was stabilized through most of the Colonial and National periods with a median age of 16 years until it rose slightly in the census of 1820. Since 1810, the

American population has continued to grow older and the
census records steadily rising median ages: 19 years in 1850,
20 years in 1860, 25 years in 1920, and 30 years in 1950. While
the post-World War II rise in fertility caused a slight drop in
the median age, for the past 30 years it has hovered around
age 30.

Median age is demographically significant, but the proportion of elderly in a population is equally significant. Since
1900 the United States population has doubled, but the proportion of the 65-years-and-over has increased nearly seven
times. Today the nation has about 12 million women and
nearly 10 million men over 65. As of July 1, 1977 the number
of persons 60-plus years old became 32.9 million or 15.2% of
the resident population. This age group has increased twice as
fast since 1970 as the total population. Moreover, the baby
boom of the 1950s will be the gray boom of the 2010s.

Not only are more Americans growing older but "older"
Americans are growing older. The 75-plus population has
grown numerically ten times, and the 85-plus group has increased around 17 times since 1900. Census projections indicate that by the year 2035 the 75-plus group will be more than
a third of the past-65 population; the 85-plus group 1 of every
10. If longer life expectancy is an outstanding achievement of
our times, it has brought with it critical social questions about
meeting the needs of the elderly and resolving them in harmony
with the needs of the rest of society.

Among other things, the 1970s will be remembered as the
decade when the academic world discovered gerontology. The
medical and health professions were not much earlier in pio-
neering the field of care for the elderly which we now call *geriatrics*. The *Oxford English Dictionary*, published in 1933, does
not even list either *geriatrics* or *gerontology* anywhere in its 12
volumes. Every other stage of the life cycle had at least begun
to be carefully studied and ingeniously classified by scholars
and scientists. The human species was somehow an attractive
object for study through conception, gestation, birth, baby-

hood, childhood, puberty, adolescence, and young adulthood. But approaching what is now said to be the mature years, interest seemed to disappear.

In America, one of the first social scientists to show serious interest in aging was G. Stanley Hall who published the treatise *Senescene* in 1972. Possibly if World War II (1941-45) had not intervened, some of the momentum of Roosevelt's New Deal would have kept aging and the elderly more prominent in the nation's social reform agenda. As it turned out, gerontology did not achieve any wide scale popularity as a topic for study until the late 1940s. For the last 30 years a scattering of centers or institutes across the land have struggled for existence, and a few universities have offered some kind of special preparation for career work on aging. In the past few years, however, gerontology has had the push of federal funds, has grown at an astonishing rate, and has become a field of study on many campuses and professional schools. The first edition of the *National Directory of Educational Programs in Gerontology* (1976) indicated that 1275 academic institutions were offering at least a single course in aging. An equally clear indicator of society's new attitude toward aging is the growth in organizational membership for the self-identified aged. In 1961, the year of the first White House Conference on Aging, some 250,000 Americans held memberships in the various professional and consumer organizations with a particular concern within the field of aging. In 1977 that number had reached 14 million. The original national organization for professionals in the field of aging, the Gerontological Society, began in 1945 with 80 members. Now there are nearly 5000.

While a growing percentage of the total federal budget goes to persons over 65—the 1979 estimate is $112 billion or about 24%—money designated for research is miniscule. The two agencies most visible identified with gerontology are the Administration on Aging (AoA), part of the Office of Human Development in the Department of Health, Education and Welfare, and the National Institute on Aging (NIA), newest member of the 11-member National Institute of Health group. The AoA budget has escalated from $30 million six years ago to $560 million for 1979, with most of the funds earmarked for health, housing, and training programs. Approximately $59.3 million of this budget was allocated in 1979 to "Research, Training, Special Projects," but the priority here is research, rather than training and special projects. For the 1979 fiscal year, the National Institute on Aging received $56.4 million, a 61% increase from the preceding year; and the bulk of these funds are intended for research. A few other federal agencies allot monies for aging research, most notably the National Institute for Mental Health, which has a Division of Special Mental Health Programs Center on Aging, and the Veterans Administration which has been steadily expanding its research and training programs through a network of Geriatric Research, Education, and Clinical Centers (GRECC).

While the aged in society have always constituted problems at some levels, it is only recently that they have begun to represent a major *social problem*. There have always been the aged or elderly persons in communities, and they have received attention for those special disabilities associated with aging. Thus, literature and history are replete with examples of the failing monarch, the deposed family head, problems of removal and transfer of the power down generations, the pathetic, feeble old person, and so on. There is nothing new in this nor in the sentiments expressed about this life phenomenon. What constitutes the transition into a major social problem, however, is the increasing prominence that the aged have in American society. The age pyramid has changed; it has higher proportions of people who are aged. In addition, some aspects of the fluctuations of fertility trends historically lead to anticipation of even greater prominence for the aged and possibly greater problems.

It is with the increase in proportions and, commensurately, of numbers of the aged, that we have the development of highly specialized interest in gerontology and geriatrics. Geriatrics is the branch of medicine dealing with medical problems associated with age; but it is difficult to define the bounds of such a specialty. In a broad sense, thus, since medicine is largely oriented towards the maintenance of life, many aspects of specialties will focus interest up the age pyramid. The advance of medicine itself, however, alters specialties so that interest that may have been more associated with the aged becomes of more general interest. If, for example, the communicative diseases are virtually eliminated, then, in general, the causes for dying will have to be bodily malfunction and failure. Thus the young and the aged become more similar, and the difference may simply be one of probability of involvement in malfunctions. Concepts that might seem clear become murky as people begin to examine them more carefully.

Several of the contributors to this book have illustrated the narrowness of knowledge on which we build our theories and myths about aging. Carl Eisdorfer presents some striking examples of invalid generalizations regarding the supposed cognitive decline among the elderly which were not due to normal aging itself. These deficits were caused by a childhood illness that affected a special cohort and only appeared when the group reached old age. Here lies a constant challenge to the gerontological researcher. Developmental changes, whether biomedical, social, or behavioral, must be carefully scrutinized to determine whether they are intrinsic to aging itself or if they arise from individual and group characteristics.

What makes aging and the aged a social problem is its recognition by society as an important aspect of behavior that needs attention. This recognition, of course, is due to questions of scale and cost to the society; but equally it must be viewed as something which may emanate from the self-interest and militancy of those who need the attention. The social problem becomes more important if viewed by legislators, for example, in terms of the voting consequences of ignoring the problem. Legislators must respond to their constituencies to be returned to government, and thus the cycle of interest is relatively simple to discern.

The facts of the increasing numbers and portions of aged are quite visible, and dealing with these population shifts becomes a major concern for planning. Presumably, planning is to be based on facts as known and in terms of potential consequences of policies when actually placed in effect. To occur, the description of facts not only needs to be accurate, but it must also examine the relevant variables appropriate for the description of the social phenomenon. The aged are not isolated; they are a part of the fabric of society.

How the aged operate in society—their needs and the types of services that may be provided for them—requires attention by social science. It is not sufficient merely to inventory the statistics about the aged; it is necessary to describe reasonably the operation of the society as a whole so that the consequences in those demographic changes that have been observed and are anticipated may be reasonably projected. It becomes essential to have an overview of the basic facts about the aging population, the aged, and society more generally, as it impinges on the problems of the aged. To satisfy such an objective is more than the several handbooks on aging have been able to do. We are still at a point where much knowledge is anecdotal and research seems to accumulate by the paper-weight of studies rather than by the findings. In this context it is vital to emphasize the state of the art, the research perspectives, the interplay of theory and fact, and those points needing additional attention and clarification. The essays in this book are brief and selective, not encyclopedic. It is the intent to stimulate interest and thought on some more central issues than to solve all the problems at once. After all, if we did solve them all, what would the gerontologists have to do?

ECONOMIC
PERSPECTIVES

1

ECONOMIC ROLES AND
THE STATUS OF THE ELDERLY

Charlotte F. Muller

Life expectancy provides a framework to consider the economic conditions of the elderly. Dramatic increases in life expectancy occurred in the United States between 1900 and
1960, and improvements continued after 1960. In 1975 the
average expected life for a person just born was 72.5 years.
Within this average, men had less life expectancy than women,
and whites had more than all other races (Table 1). Persons
already 65 could expect to live an average of 16.0 years more
(DHEW, 1977: 5-4). For individuals, survival and planning
for old age are uncertain, for 25.4% of those born in 1975
would not reach 65, and 46.6% would not reach 75 (DHEW,
1977: 5-8). At the same time, those reaching 65 face a long
period of life in which economic needs and resources must be
balanced. Other probabilities besides survival per se are involved. A high proportion of women are divorced or widowed
before retirement age. As of 1975, the proportion amounted to

one-third of all women aged 46-60 who were ever married. Less than one-third of divorced women receive support from ex-husbands (DHEW, 1978).

Social planning is able to deal with these uncertainties because actuarial principles can be applied. Both voluntary and compulsory funds may be used. Voluntary funds such as pension plans and individual annuities appeal to those seeking to avoid risks. Through compulsory funds, such as social security for narrow or broad groups of workers in a country, however, those individuals who enjoy risk or are not responsive to it as a threat, and those who live with unwanted risk because their incomes are too low for current needs, can receive protection.

In discussing the economic aspects of aging, the subjects of economic roles, economic status or levels, and policy issues can be separated for convenience. In actuality, they are closely intertwined. For example, role opportunities influence income levels and public policy decisions about social security benefit levels, compulsory retirement and the like, affect both roles and status of the elderly.

Another close interrelation exists between individuals' opportunities and experience in earlier years of life and their economic positions in old age. For example, both desire and ability to save for old age affect assets after retirement, and

TABLE 1   Life Expectancy by Race and Sex, 1975

	White		All Other		
Per 100,000 born alive	Male	Female	Male	Female	Overall
Alive at age 20	97,015	98,033	95,611	96,772	97,270
Alive at age 65	69,386	83,204	54,349	71,484	74,593
Percentage surviving to 65	71.52	84.87	56.84	73.87	76.69
Alive at 85	15,822	35,025	13,326	27,365	24,543
Percentage surviving 65-85	22.80	42.10	24.35	38.28	32.90

Source: DHEW, 1977: 5-11.

early choice of occupation affects freedom to continue work at will in old age. At the same time, responsibility for intergenerational transfers to the aged through the family and through the tax system influences the ability of younger persons to prepare for their own old age. Many, perhaps most, important policy issues regarding the elderly involve the extent of desired redistribution of national income among age groups and the most effective ways of bringing it about. The fact that employer contributions toward retirement are, through the workings of the market, eventually paid by workers themselves emphasizes that real sacrifices are involved in social provision for retirement.

ECONOMIC ROLES

The economic roles of the elderly are important in a variety of ways. They determine possible income flows, they establish the individual in society, they involve meaningful use of time, and they preserve a range of personal options. Elderly persons may participate in the economy as producers of market services. In 1975 over 4 million family heads age 65 +—3,354,000 males and 692,000 females—derived some income from earnings, as did over a million unrelated individuals—335,000 males and 862,000 females (U.S., Bureau of the Census, 1977: 143-148).[1]

Elderly persons may also produce nonmarket services, including those intimately relating to consumption, such as meal preparation, mending and small repairs of household goods, major maintenance of both owned and rented residences, and volunteer services for the benefit of others.

Although nonmarket services entering personal or family real income are difficult to measure, they may be an important component of the living standard. Two needs connected with nonmarket activities are: (1) assistance when health is impaired; and (2) improving efficiency through social support services such as health education and consumer advice. Current efforts to establish a benefit right under social security for those women who enter old age with little qualifying employment, but with years as homemakers and mothers, would recognize nonmarket services. For the elderly, services rendered to children and grandchildren may facilitate the participation of younger persons in the labor market, and may also be part of nonmarket exchanges in which children provide maintenance or personal services to the elderly.

Elderly persons can also participate in the economy as property owners. But aside from residential property, this role is rarely a major one. In 1967 only 16-18% of aged "units" —couples or unrelated individuals—had more than 20% of their income from assets. Recipients amounted to more than half of married couples and about 40% of the others (DHEW, Social Security Administration, 1973).

Residential ownership is far more common than investments. In 1969 the proportion of nonfarm families with aged heads who were homeowners was 71%. The figure increased from 59% a decade earlier, and the rate of increase was higher than for nonaged families (Chen, 1971). Owning a house has both advantages and disadvantages. It makes a significant contri-

TABLE 2   Proportion with 20% or More of Income
           from Assets

	All Aged		Nonbeneficiaries	
	All	Recipients Only	All	Recipients Only
Married Couples	16%	30%	8%	16%
Nonmarried Men	16%	40%	13%	– –
Nonmarried Women	18%	43%	10%	38%
Number of units (000)				
Married	4,363	2,279	472	224
Nonmarried Men	1,942	753	244	– –
Nonmarried Women	5,778	2,382	902	251

bution to the net worth of the aged and toward real (as distinguished from money) income, but real income is not subject to discretionary reallocation by the individual. Many elderly persons are "overhoused" in relation to current family size, while the costs of house maintenance have risen with inflation. Some states give property tax concessions to aged taxpayers. One policy goal of such subsidies is the occupancy of owned homes, but it raises a number of questions which involve equity within, as well as between, age groups. As to equity within the aged, is it satisfied when a homeowner has lighter taxes than a renter? If not, is this justified because of social advantages in promoting home ownership and retention of homes? Is it clear that the tax subsidy is an appropriate and sufficient incentive for such a purpose? As to equity between older and younger owners, is there a fair treatment of those in like circumstances when the tax burden on residences is lighter regardless of the relative incomes of the individuals? These are examples of the types of questions involved in such subsidies.

Expenditures on home maintenance come out of the aged person's budget, and this brings us to one of the major economic roles of the elderly—that of consumer. The ability of aged persons to function as consumers to their own satisfaction depends on a number of factors. If they are out of the labor market, they have more time to acquire market information and compare prices and quality. They usually have less physical mobility, however, and some are unable to own cars. Smaller quantities of goods are needed because households are smaller, but for some products, buying in small quantities is more expensive.

The contribution of aged persons to effective demand for the products and services of the economy depends on their income. The incentive to save is reduced, and indeed dissaving—spending more than current income—may occur if income is inadequate and if urgent needs arise. Of course, the contribution to total demand from retirement benefits is offset by a transfer from younger age groups who are taxed to finance benefits currently authorized. If the income of the aged is from employment, their competition for jobs in a slack economy is not welcomed.

The consumer role is thus intertwined with recognition of a productive role for the aged, and both involve equity considerations; that is, how can one group be protected in employment and buying power without injury to the other, and can this be done without advantage to individuals in one group who may be in better economic positions than individuals in the other?

Some of the consumption by aged persons is mediated by group or institutional buyers. For example, health care is financed through prepayment. Buying groups of aged have been formed to improve bargaining power. Aged persons who enter the institutionalized population become indirect consumers without autonomy in the market. (Table 3 shows aged persons in health facilities on temporary and permanent bases). They are converted into clients, part of a population that constitutes a form of asset for a variety of service agencies and proprietary organizations. Because of services they need, aged persons provide the raison d'être, or part of it, for organizations providing institutional health care, home health services, social services, group activities, pension administration services, and so on.

One social policy issue that results is inadequate services for the elderly. Client status may also lead to orienting the range of options and the style of provision toward preserving or maximizing captive client populations rather than to helping them achieve greater autonomy and status. The extent to which the motives of providers and of recipients diverge can be seen in the nursing home market—nominally under regulation, but at the worst deteriorating into a real estate market with revenue-generating aged persons attached to the property like serfs to the manor.

In our discussion of economic roles, we have now traveled the range from full economic activity to passive and exploited

TABLE 3   Aged Persons in Health-Related Facilities

A. As residents			
Chronic disease hospitals		1970	35,192
Tuberculosis hospitals			5,608
Nursing homes		1973-1974	
65-74	163,100		
75-84	384,900		
85+	413,600		
	Total		961,600
Psychiatric halfway houses		1971	400
Alcoholic halfway houses		1971	100

B. As "episode" users		Discharges or episodes
State and county mental hospitals	1971	133,700
Private mental hospitals	1971	12,400
Veterans psychiatric hospitals	1973-1974	6,900
Psychiatric units of short-stay hospitals	1971	36,100
Department of Defense hospitals	1973	10,012
Indian Health Service hospitals	1973-1974	6,500
VA-general medical and surgical hospitals	1973-1974	152,800
Short-stay hospitals	1973	6,937,200
Community mental health centers (Federally-funded)	1971	9,200

Source: U.S. Department of Health, Education and Welfare (1976) The Nation's Use of Health Resources. Washington, DC: Government Printing Office.

dependency. Policy options can be framed in terms of which roles to emphasize, and how to do so.

ECONOMIC STATUS

To turn to a review of the economic status of the elderly, we first look at the distribution of poverty, and then examine the major factors that determine economic status in old age: Social Security, supplemental pensions, and employment. Health status is also significant, since both the need for intensive health services and the management of severely disabling, chronic ailments are important threats to economic status. The uneven distribution of the rights to income from the three major sources noted, and the unfavorable economic position of those with impaired health status, stand out upon review of available statistics.

In a discussion of income sources of the aged, earned income refers only to what is derived from current labor (or professional) services. Nonearned income from Social Security and pension plans is based on previous earnings. Income from investments is another form of nonearned income even though common usage refers to "earnings" on financial assets. Transfer payments based on need (Supplemental Security Income) are nonearned income also. Thus nonearned income covers the range from the very rich to the very poor.

The poverty index was developed in 1964 and is based on the cost of an economy-level food budget equal to one-third of the total budget for a family of 3 or more, and 27% for a couple. For a couple with the man at 65, the poverty level of income was $2,985 in 1974, but this is an extreme definition of poverty resulting in an underestimate of the number of aged poor. The Bureau of Labor Statistics low-level retired-couple budget was $4,228 and the intermediate budget $6,041.

If the conservative notion of poverty is used, nationwide figures on poverty can be misleading for a given area. The cost of a retired couple's budget in a given area can be well above the national average, but benefits under law are not adjusted to the local cost of living.[2] For example, Boston, New York, Hartford, and other cities were well above average urban costs of an intermediate budget ($6,738 in autumn 1976), whereas Baton Rouge, Orlando, and Dallas were well below (Bienstock, 1978: 12).

In addition, individual couples may have to spend a great deal for a particular budget item so that their budgetary need is not reflected in a typical or standard budget. This is especially dramatic for medical care, but could also apply to transportation, special diet, or housing.

The number of aged with incomes below the poverty level fell from 5.6 million in 1959 to 3.3 million in 1974 (from 37.7% to 15.7%). This was the result of expansion and liberalization of public and private pensions. Furthermore, in-kind benefits not included in money income figures rose. Relative to younger age groups, however, the income of the elderly is not adequate.

In 1975, persons 65 and over in poverty numbered 2,634,000 whites and 652,000 blacks. There were 1.0 million males and 2.3 million females, or about 3.3 million persons in all. The poverty rate was 11.4% for men and 18.1% for women, and was higher for both sexes among unrelated individuals than for those living in families. The rates for unrelated individuals were 27.7% for all males and 31.9% for all females. Sex and race had an influence; the rates were 23.8% for white males, 29.1% for white females, 51.8% for black males and 65.8% for black females. The 400,000 male and 1.7 million female unrelated individuals represented by these rates made up 70% of the aged poor.

If income is expressed as a percentage of the poverty level, then of the 21,662,000 persons aged 65+ in 1975, 442,000 were under 50% of the poverty level, 801,000 between 50% and 74% of it, and 2,073,000 were between 75% and 99% of poverty level income. However, an additional 4.3 million were in brackets just above the poverty level of income.

Farm dwellers were only slightly more likely to be in poverty than nonfarm dwellers, but there were strong regional differences; the poverty rate for the aged was especially high in the South and even more so for southern blacks (46.3%). The rate was higher in nonmetropolitan compared to metropolitan areas, and in central cities compared to other locations within metropolitan areas. Within "poverty areas" the rate was 29.1% compared to 11.0% in other areas.

Marital status correlates with poverty rates. Among unrelated individuals, widowed women have a rate of 62.1%, almost double the rate for singles. Men who are separated are more likely to be poor than those who are widowed or divorced.

INCOME SOURCES

Of 8,163,000 families with an aged head of household, there are 4.0 million with earned income, of whom 3.4 million derive it from wages and salaries rather than self-employment. In all, 7.4 million receive Social Security, about 900,000 get public assistance or Supplemental Security Income (SSI) and 1 million get other transfer payments. Property income is received by 5.3 million, and pensions other than Social Security, alimony, and annuities are received by 3.1 million. An average of 2.7 types of income are received.

Of 6,851,000 unrelated individuals, 1.2 million have earned income, 6.2 million have social security, 950,000 get SSI, about 600,000 get other transfers, 3.7 million have property income, and 1.7 million have pensions, alimony, and so forth.

SOCIAL SECURITY

Not many people are able to allocate income over a lifetime because information about the worth of different options is imperfect, certainty about the future is lacking, and the length of retirement has been increasing. Collective retirement plans enable society to carry out its commitment to replace the extended family, and enable the individual to avoid the stream of uncertainties facing the choice of a savings rate and its attainment.

The federal Social Security program, initiated in 1935, is described as a compulsory intergenerational transfer system to deal with income maintenance in old age. To examine its adequacy, we draw on the Continuous Work History Sample of the SSA, a 1% longitudinal sample of persons with covered employment, taken from reporting forms and records used in program administration. What follows is based on retired and disabled workers on the benefit rolls at the end of 1972. The covered earnings determine eventual benefits through a computation in which the worst earning years are discarded. (All earning years, however, are considered in establishing that the required quarters of coverage have been satisfied).

Sexual comparisons show that women had lower benefits than men. The primary insurance amount is affected by (1) starting work at the beginning of adult life rather than later; (2) stopping work at a later rather than earlier age; (3) continuity of employment; and (4) earnings levels. These may be interrelated. Discontinuous work histories and low earnings may be associated, and could produce a low earning history; early retirement is found with poorer earnings records (Thompson, 1977). The details of the sexual comparison follow, showing the impact on benefits of differences in lifetime earning levels.

In 1972 15.5 million retired persons were on the social security rolls—8.9 million men and 6.6 million women—but only 14.6 million received benefits because the rest had enough earnings to offset benefits due. Men had longer coverage—65% began before 1941, and 17% between 1941 and 1950. Comparable figures for women were 41% and 34%. The percentage of men with a start before 1941 would have been even higher if more men survived to retirement. As it was, 63% of men but only 38% of women had 20+ years of covered work. Women who started in covered jobs in the same year as men had fewer covered quarters, and even those women with the same years and quarters as men tended to have lower lifetime earnings; for those with the most extended coverage in years, 40% of men but only 13% of women had covered earnings of $80,000+. The result was smaller primary insurance amounts: for those with

at least 30 years, 84% of men but only 51% of women had a
Primary Insured Amount (PIA) of $200+ per month.

Race comparisons are also available. They show that 2 of
every 3 white, retired men had some earnings credits before
1941, while the figure for black men is slightly less; this is
explained by lower longevity of blacks. Among retired women,
43% of the whites but only 22% of the blacks had their first
credits before 1941. That more black women than white
women got first credits after 1950 is partly due to the extension
of coverage to domestic workers.

Overall, white workers have higher PIAs and higher lifetime
covered earnings than other races.

For workers with credits before 1941 and 80-119 quarters
of coverage, 70% of the white men had PIA's of $200 or more
but only 43% of the black men did so. The Primary Insured
Amount is under $200 for 50% of men 62-64, 41% of those who
are 65-71, 50% between 72-79, and 71% for age 80 and over.
Similar figures for women are: 84%, 75%, 83% and 93%.

PENSIONS

Pensions are societal because they are (1) regulated by the
government, and (2) subsidized through preferential tax treatment. The private industrial pension plan is an important
source of retirement income, but it is uneven in its effects on
the economic status of individuals. Private pension coverage
expanded from 9.8 million workers in 1950 to 26.1 million in
1970. Following dramatic growth in the 1950s, the 1960s saw
a liberalizing of benefit formulas, vesting requirements, and
the mandatory retirement age. Many workers, however, are
uncovered or never collect benefits. This is due to restrictive
vesting and service requirements, withdrawal of contributions
on leaving the job, and bankruptcy of firms and their pension
plans.

The passage of the Employee Retirement Income Security Act (ERISA) in 1974 guaranteed vesting rights for employer contributions even if all employee contributions are withdrawn when changing jobs. Under vesting, a worker does not lose rights to a retirement income upon leaving a job in a firm with a pension plan; benefits are deferred until retirement age is reached. Vesting was spreading voluntarily before ERISA, but was reported by only one-third of the workers with coverage in 1972. To satisfy requirements under the law, full vesting after 10 years (and other options) may be used by employers. While these are beneficial to workers, there is concern that the growth of pension plans will be deterred by ERISA's complex requirements. Since likelihood of vesting depends on job tenure, wage level, and, particularly, industrial/occupational categories, vesting is related to other features of pension adequacy that vary across categories of workers.

Pension portability through multiemployer networks allows reciprocity of pension rights. This is a fast-growing form of pension organization. The number of workers who were covered this way in 1973 was 7.5 million, equal to one-third of all covered workers in 1970. A few large plans cover most of the participants (44 plans have over one-half, and 10 plans have one-third, of all workers). Portability is found with multi-employer collective bargaining and overcomes limitations due to small firms, seasonal or irregular employment, and frequent job changes. A drawback of these plans is that they do limit the freedom to work anywhere in the industry.

Figures on pension adequacy come from the Retirement History Survey, which studies pension coverage and receipt of pensions in relation to the longest job held. Most pensions use earnings history and not terminal income as a base, and therefore length of work life is critical in evaluating the benefit level. Of those persons who were in the private sector on their longest job, 49% of men and 21% of women had pension coverage. For men, rates were higher for manufacturing and professional service industrial groups, professional and clerical occupations, those with 21+ years on the longest job, and those earning $7,500 and over. If they were still employed on the longest job in 1969, the coverage rate was higher. The trends were similar for women, except that the best industries were transportation, communication, and public utilities. But women were more likely than men to have had job characteristics associated with low coverage, and, in addition, their coverage was less than men's within each category. For instance, in manufacturing, 63% of men but only 31% of women were covered. For men and women with similar industry, occupation, salary, length of service, and continued tenure in 1969, the rates for the most advantaged group were 61-62% coverage.

When the probability of coverage was analyzed by multiple correlation, earnings were less important than other factors just described. But the proportion of variance explained (R^2) varies from .35 to .49 for different categories, showing that other still unidentified factors contribute to coverage rate.[3]

In 1972, 72% of men who were covered by a private pension but had no earnings in that year received benefits, as did 55% of the women. These low rates were not explained by absence of early retirement options under pension plans, since the rates were not higher for those aged 65-66 compared to those under 65.

The sources of pensions for government workers vary. Federal employees have their own retirement plan, and no dual coverage with Social Security is allowed. For state and local employees, dual coverage is not precluded, and about 58% of personnel have it. However, 8% of state and local employees do not have coverage through a retirement plan other than Social Security.

Twenty-six percent of the men and 42% of the women who had pension coverage in private industry received only Social Security benefits; similar figures for government workers were

11% for federal civilian employees and 19% for state and local employees. Reasons for this include termination of service before vesting, withdrawal of contributions by workers on leaving a job, and temporary work status.

Of all non-earners aged 61-66 in 1972—summing public and private employees—only 48% of the men and 21% of the women received dual retirement benefits.

The median income from pensions was, for men, $4,290 for government workers and $2,230 for private workers. For women the amounts were $3,650 and $1,200. The reason for the sexual difference in private employment pensions is difference in earnings, because length of service among recipients was the same.

The theory that federal Social Security will be supplemented by pension income—and at adequate levels—is not a reality for many retired persons. ERISA will improve the situation for many currently employed.

EARNINGS FROM EMPLOYMENT

Flexible retirement has been adopted by many countries and permits individual health, working conditions, labor market opportunities, and the like to influence retirement age. A review of seven industrial countries[4] shows that this first developed (in the 1960s) usually because of arduous or hazardous jobs, but later (in the 1970s) early retirement was offered to relieve unemployment, and a combination of partial pensions with part-time employment was added as a retirement option. But the fiscal problems in the governmental retirement systems in these countries discouraged expansion of programs that would offer such options.

In the industrial countries studied, the first social security schemes could not estimate pension costs under alternative age limits for working life. Although census data showed age-

specific labor force participation and life expectancy, there
was nothing to show how many workers would leave if a
pension were offered. This uncertainty predisposed the legis-
lating of a high starting age. However, this conflicted with the
aim of reducing poverty among the aged. Often it was hoped
that reducing the retirement age would protect older workers,
who might be out of touch with technological change and are
at greater risk of ill health, by offering an alternative to re-
maining in the labor market.

Although 65 was the customary pension age, it was clearly
too rigid. A worker might have impaired health without
qualifying for disability benefits. A reduced pension at an
earlier age enabled a worker to leave. Other workers with short
earnings records were allowed to stay at work longer to earn
minimum benefits. When labor shortages existed, the image of
older workers was deliberately beautified. Retirement was
later stimulated by raising benefit levels either by tying them
to price or wage levels, or by changing the formula to reflect
more recent earnings, and real income benefits in the form of
health care services were offered. For these seven countries,
flexibility is oriented more to early than to late retirement:
Only 6-7% of those aged 65+ are in the labor force.

In the United States in past years, compulsory retirement
in industry and Social Security worked together to dislodge
many employed persons from their jobs at age 65. A substantial number of these elderly reenter the labor market but they
do not compete for the same types of job they previously held.
Instead they augment the available pool of candidates for less
desirable and less remunerative jobs. Some of the postretirement jobs yield so little that persons on Social Security may
continue on benefit status; or, from another viewpoint, Social
Security made possible a labor market for part-time work. In
other cases, a private pension ekes out earnings, but the
person does not file for federal benefits.

A flexible early option for retirement with a reduced Social
Security benefit before age 65 was first offered to women,

many of whom had a poor earnings outlook in their sixties. The rationale offered was that the typical age difference between husband and wife made joint retirement more likely if this option were used. (Today the age difference between spouses is narrowing, and more women have continuous work records.) The option was soon extended, however, to men and tended to be used by those who had disabilities or trouble finding work. The 1978 law (effective January 1, 1979) shifts the minimum age for forced retirement to 70, at which time the retirement test (i.e., a cap on permitted earnings) ceases to apply.

As it is easier to keep a job than to look for a new one, this law will probably raise the labor force participation rate after age 65. At the present time those who do work after 65 can add to their earnings records on which benefits are figured. This is advantageous to those with less adequate employment histories. As Medicare starts at age 65 regardless of employment status, it is not an incentive either to stop or to continue work. (Copayments and uncovered services, however, stimulate the desire for earned income.) Tax privileges and other subsidies start at age 65 or earlier regardless of employment status.

In 1974, 10.4 million workers—about 45% of the workers in defined benefit plans—had mandatory retirement at 65 or later and many were in plans with forced *early* retirement. Under some plans a worker cannot be kept on and under others an employer can extend further employment on a year-to-year basis. Automatic retirement (with no extension option) usually applied at age 68. In some of the plans with forced early retirement, a worker with 25 (or 30) years of service receives extra benefits if dismissed, but in others the benefit is no greater than the regular early retirement benefit (Kittner, 1977).

Among aged males in families, over half have no earned income; among female heads of household about two-fifths are in this position. For unrelated individuals, no earned income is reported by 77% of males and 83% of females. Overall, 56.6% of males and 75.3% of females in these categories have no reported earnings. For male heads of household, income levels are highest for those with both earned and nonearned incomes, next highest for earned incomes only, and lowest for those without earnings. For other categories, those who have only earnings are too few for averages to be computed, but in each case incomes average more for those with both earned and nonearned income. The percentage of family units in poverty is 15.2% for those with earned income only, and 12.6% for those with nonearned income only, but drops to 4.7% for those with both sources of income.

Employment of the elderly is influenced by *changes* in the labor market, social security, and retirement practices superimposed on fairly *stable* characteristics of these three social institutions. For this reason interpretation—or even a description—of the elderly in relation to the labor market based on single-year data is continually subject to correction or revision.

Older workers tend to be less mobile both geographically and occupationally. For example, only 5.5% of all persons moving to a different standard metropolitan statistical area (March 1975-March 1977) were 65 or over, although the aged were about 11% of the whole population at that time. The proportion of workers 65 or over changing occupations was 1.7% for men and 2.5% for women, and in the ages 55-64, the proportions were 2.6% and 2.4%—representing a drop from younger ages (Bienstock, 1978).

The 1975-1977 employment rates for those past 65 showed much more intrayear variability than for all persons. Also, the current duration of unemployment is much longer—29.1 weeks average in March 1978 compared with 16.9 weeks at age 45-54, for example (Bienstock, 1978). Many older persons leave the labor force (or stay out, once having left) because they think they cannot obtain work. This was the leading reason offered for not looking for work in 1977 (36.6% of the aged offered this reason, double the percentage for all ages). The labor force participation rate drops with the advancing age. For men it drops from 87.1% at age 55 to 75.3% at age 60, 36.6% at age 65, and 22.3% at age 69. For women the drop is from 50.2% at age 55, to 41.6% at age 60, 19.1% at age 65, and 11.9% at age 69. Figures over a period of years for both men and women show a rise in the proportion taking early retirement at reduced benefits: by 1974, 46.4% of the men and 64.6% of the women retired in this fashion (Bienstock, 1978).

HEALTH STATUS

The interrelation of health status and economic status is especially noteworthy in old age. Low income recipients are less able to afford good nutrition, safe housing with proper control of temperature and humidity, and needed health services. Persons in poor health use more health services in and out of the hospital. They can be obliged to draw on savings to meet the costs (even under Medicare) of copayment, deductible, uncovered services, and charges by physicians in excess of Medicare-allowed charges. For those under 65, Medicare is available if a disabled worker benefit has been authorized—446,000 men and 194,000 women aged 60-64 were in this category in 1972 (Lingg, 1977). For others aged 60-64, Medicaid (public assistance medical care) supplements private resources and insurance.

Income level is negatively associated with health level as indicated by chronic limitations and disability days (Table 4). In these data, however, the percentages of aged persons using physician and hospital services show few relations to income. Other sources indicate that persons with the highest incomes do use more services per person than most other groups. Hence, use does not match need. Nevertheless, chronic illness is a powerful factor in use and accompanying expenses. Per-

TABLE 4   Health and Health Care Indicators for
           Persons Aged 65+ by Income

	% with doctor visits in past year (1)	% with short stay hospital episode in past year (2)	% with limitations (3)	Restricted activity days per person (4)
Income ($000)				
Under 5.0	79.7	18.9	53.4	50.3
5.0-9.9	80.6	18.4	43.1	36.4
10.0-14.9	81.2	18.6	39.6	31.5
15+	81.2	19.2	38.7	28.0

Source: National Center for Health Statistics.

sons with some activity limitations number 39.3% of the aged.
They constitute 3.9% of the whole population but use 8.0% of
all office visits, 7.0% of all hospital discharges, and 11.9% of
all hospital days. In addition, they make up most of the nursing
home population, a group for which 3.4 chronic conditions
per resident have been reported (DHEW, 1976, 1974). Other
figures show high rates of multiple conditions among the aged,
entailing longer stays in the hospital and more expense.

Aged persons in the upper half of the income distribution
tend to have supplementary private hospital coverage to pick
up costs not covered by Medicare. Hence protection against
economic risks of illness is correlated with other measures of
economic status.

POLICY ISSUES

Major policy issues concerning the economics of aging
involve the Social Security system, the private pension system,
the participation of the elderly in the labor market, the tax
system, and the use of general revenues to improve the position
of the elderly.

One major Social Security issue is how much of the income of the aged should be derived from a universal public program. Private pensions vary from one place of employment to another and by occupational level and have other limitations. Hence the public program is more likely to provide uniformity of protection unless private pensions are placed under more regulation. But the tax rate required to increase the share of public benefits in total retirement income reduces the disposable income of economically active age groups—an obvious deterrent to passing the needed legislation. Younger persons may support such laws if they perceive a benefit to themselves in later years, or if they foresee relief from obligations for aged parents (depending on whether legislative changes apply to current retirees).

Another Social Security issue is the extent to which benefits should be wage-related (Henle, 1972). Protection for the poor is attained by weakening an element in the reward structure for labor. Some of the poor have had long earnings records at low wages; others have a more marginal attachment to the labor market. Another major concern relates to women whose length of service in the household has hitherto had no standing with regard to Social Security except as filtered through a spouse.

Other Social Security issues concern the level of wage replacement achieved by benefits (of critical interest in each person's retirement decision, as well as for the prevention of poverty) and the commitment of the system to adjusting the benefits of current beneficiaries to cost of living changes and to rising expectations based on productivity.

Although the spouse benefit allows 99.4% replacement for a low-income worker retiring at 65, replacement is only 53% in absence of this benefit (for a worker retiring at age 62). The Social Security replacement rate falls rapidly as earning record rises. A worker with *median* taxable earnings in each year could never reach a 71% income replacement rate (considered to equal parity). The average is 46.2%. For a worker with *maximum* earnings only 33% is replaced (Clark, 1977).

One of the controversies regarding the Social Security system is based on the claim that it reduces savings and, therefore, the potential for national economic growth. To diminish the effect of this claim, it has been noted that, although the growth of output is indeed related to the growth of real capital, growth in skills and knowledge is another, and even more important, source of output growth; also, empirical studies do not show a clear relation between savings and capital formation (Lesnoy and Hambor, 1975).

Analysis of saving by individuals in an economy that includes Social Security is based on an extended life-cycle theory of consumption. According to this theory, saving smoothes out the stream of lifetime consumption by shifting personal spending from working life to retirement; Social Security rights modify the necessity of doing so (Feldstein, 1976). It has been recognized that even theoretically this does not imply that savings are reduced by the public programs. An interest in retiring at a lower age becomes an intervening variable. Workers who retire at an early age would have to reduce consumption to make this possible.

Social Security Administration economists have reviewed the work in this area and have concluded that there is no clear-cut evidence that having Social Security benefit rights lowers individual savings (Esposito, 1978). It is recognized, however, that the effect of Social Security contributions and benefits on macroeconomic trends is a very significant aspect of Social Security tax and benefit policy.

With or without Social Security, current retirees are inevitably supported by the economically active population. Browning has concluded from this that current workers gain something if the system exists, since it establishes their legal claim to future benefits without the uncertainties and limitations of alternative means of establishing future income rights in the private sector.

In bargaining for private pensions there is a competition for priority between wages (and wage supplements) immediately accessible to younger workers (e.g., fertility-related health care) and more adequate pension plans. This involves a choice for each person (wages now vs. future income) and each group (younger workers vs. those approaching retirement). At the social level, several improvements need to be analyzed concerning the costs of each and who pays for it: (1) pension adequacy and equity through higher benefit level; (2) early vesting (a permanent right to accumulations financed by the employer regardless of later changes in employment; and (3) more portability (the right to add to the retirement accumulation in each subsequent job).

Policy concerning the participation of the elderly in the labor market involves relations to Social Security, supplementary pensions, manpower policy, and the tax structure. The success of the benefit structure in supporting individual choices, such as adapting retirement to health or psychological preferences, reversibility of the retirement decision, graded retirement, and shift to a different industry or occupation, should be monitored and translated into policy recommendations. Possible methods of subsidizing work force participation by the elderly—such as exempting "aged" payroll from various taxes, exempting it from fringe benefit obligations under collective bargaining, part-payment of wages, assistance to employers for project and job development, and individual retraining—need to be explored.

NOTES

1. While the word "heads" refers to various federal statistics on the aged, future census statistics will not use it. It has been rejected following criticism by social scientists and feminists for both its technical and ideological biases.

2. There may be some rough matching of benefits and area consumer prices because earnings records are tied to the local economy. There are, however, many intervening variables.

3. The equation $R^2 = 1.0$ would mean that there was no unexplained variance.

4. The countries are Denmark, Japan, Norway, Germany, France, Austria, Belgium, Switzerland, and the United Kingdom.

REFERENCES

BIENSTOCK, H. (1978) " Some facts relating to the graying of America." Presented at the Yeshiva University Conference on Aging, June 1.

CHEN, Y-P. (1971) Income: Background Issues, The Technical Committee on Aging. Report prepared for the White House Conference on Aging, Washington, DC, March.

CLARK, R. (1977) The Role of Private Pensions in Maintaining Living Standards in Retirement. NPA Report 154. Washington: National Planning Association.

ESPOSITO, L. (1978) "Effect of Social Security on saving: review of studies using U.S. time-series data." Social Security Bulletin (May): 9-17.

FELDSTEIN, M. (1976) "Social Security and saving: the extended life cycle theory." Papers and Proceedings of the 88th Annual Meeting of the American Economic Association, May, 77-86.

HAANES-OLSEN, L. (1978) "Earnings-replacement rate of old-age benefits, 1965-1975." Social Security Bulletin (January): 3-14.

HENLE, P. (1972) "Recent trends in retirement benefits related to earnings." Monthly Labor Review (June): 12-20.

KITTNER, D. R. (1977) "Forced retirement: how common is it?" Monthly Labor Review (June): 60-62.

LESNOY, S. D. AND J. C. HAMBOR (1975) "Social Security, saving, and capital formation." Social Security Bulletin (July).

LINGG, B. A. (1977) "Lifetime covered earnings and quarters of coverage of retired and disabled workers." Social Security Bulletin (October): 3-16.

SNEE, J. and M. ROSS (1978) "Social Security amendments of 1977: legislative history and summary of provisions." Social Security Bulletin (March): 3-20.

THOMPSON, G. B. (1977) "Aged women OASDI beneficiaries: income and characteristics 1971." Social Security Bulletin (April): 23-48.

——— (1978) "Pension coverage and benefits, 1972." Social Security Bulletin (February): 3-17.

U.S., Bureau of the Census (1977) "Characteristics of the population below the poverty level: 1975," CPR, Consumer Income Series P-60. Washington, DC: Government Printing Office.

U.S., Department of Health, Education and Welfare (DHEW). Health Resources Administration. National Center for Health Statistics (1977) Vital Statistics of the United States, 1975. Vol. 2, Sec. 5, Life Tables. Washington, DC: Government Printing Office.

——— (1976) "Health characteristics of persons with chronic activity limitation, United States-1974," Vital and Health Statistics Series 10, No. 112. Washington, DC: Government Printing Office.

—— (1974) "Measures of Chronic Illness Among Residents of Nursing and Professional Care Homes. United States," Vital and Health Statistics: Series 12, No. 24. Washington, DC: Government Printing Office.

U.S., Department of Health, Education and Welfare. Social Security Administration (1978) "Task force report on treatment of women under Social Security." Social Security Bulletin (May).

—— (1973) "Relative importance of income sources of the aged," ORS/SSA Research and Statistics Note, May 29. Washington, DC: Government Printing Office.

2

MORE ON THE ECONOMICS OF AGING

Abraham Monk

In her article, Professor Muller has linked major economic trends with their underlying demographic realities and even the motivational connotations of the behavior of the elderly as consumers. A number of issues that are of social policy significance, a focus which, incidentally, permeates every aspect of her paper, invite selective comment.

First, there is the issue of income maintenance. There has been a tremendous revolution in American life expectancy. One can underscore that a subpopulation of age 75 and older is growing three times faster than the group 65 to 74. Kurt Vonnegut's fascinating stories of seven or eight generation families—where the old patriarch or matriarch is age 170 or 180—may soon sound not so farfetched. But there is an overwhelming expansion of the nonproductive segment of our economy; and we behave irrationally toward it. On the one hand, the elderly are penalized for being productive through disincentives built into our Social Security system. They are also penalized by reduced incomes. Part of these inconsisten-

cies stems from our own Social Security system, the corner-
stone of all income maintenance programs for the aged. We
began our system in 1935, by literally copying the German
social security system. On the one hand, it was adopted as a
social insurance system which is contributory, with benefits
considered as a right. It was actually a form of savings or deferred earnings; but then it was assigned two parallel and inconsistent missions. One was a mechanism for intergenerational
transfers. The present working generation is thus supposed to
support the preceding working generation. But it was also
expected to reduce poverty. It appears to be doing a relatively
poor job on both counts. As an intergenerational transfer device it is jeopardizing the well-being of those paying increased
taxation at an alarming rate. And it is not, after all, lifting
older people from poverty. In fact, if income maintenance were
left to Social Security, a large number of older people would
sink deeper into poverty. Social Security does not provide a
minimum floor, and neither does it perform its intended function of social transfer.

Part of the problem is that when the German model was
copied, the United States disregarded the more popular
Danish plan of flat pensions, advocated by social action movements of the 1920s. The Townsend movement called for a universal monthly pension of $200, paid from general revenues.
Because of the limitation of the Old Age Insurance component
of Social Security, it had to be supplemented at the very beginning with the Old Age Assistance Program which was actually
a welfare program. Old Age Assistance was justified as a temporary, transitional program only for those older persons
whose primary insurance amount was low or nonexistent because of limited preceding contributions to the system. That
"temporary" system became a permanent feature until very
recently, and it has now been replaced with a euphemism, the
Supplementary Security Income program (SSI) which has also
turned into a battlefield of conflicting ideologies.

Once again, the SSI may be asked to accomplish too much. It has some novel features: It is funded from general revenues; it is noncontributory; and, it approximates a negative income tax as it established the idea of a minimum income. From a social policy point of view, these are very advanced and promising departures. But it also perpetuates many of Old Age Assistance's operational deficiences by requiring the same investigations and humiliating recertifications as any welfare program. Ultimately it does not lift people from poverty.

There is an important feature of Social Security that raises a number of agonizing questions regarding the future. Since 1975, Social Security payments have been pegged to the consumer price index. This means that Social Security is becoming a larger and larger portion of our federal tax receipts. In 1949, only 4% of all federal tax receipts were from Social Security. Now, almost 40% of all federal tax receipts are from Social Security. And if counting both the employee's and the employer's portion, more than half of the American people pay more to Social Security than to the federal income tax. This is an astounding revelation; and it explains why there is a new and great concern in policy debates about the age-dependency ratio — how many productive people it takes to support a nonproductive older person. At the time when the first cohort of older people started collecting Social Security, the ratio was about seven workers for each Social Security recipient. We are now at a point of a 3 to 1, and may well be approximating a 2 to 1 ratio. This raises the fear that we may find another Proposition 13, another revolt of taxpayers or Social Security contributors who oppose raising the Social Security tax. The productive segments of our society are wondering whether we can afford our Social Security system, and this is the message hidden in the postponement of the mandatory retirement age of 70 as of January 1979. One can favor a nonmandatory system of retirement, but remain perceptive enough to realize that the legislation in question is based only on the affordability of our economic system. It is questionable whether it will facilitate the retention of older workers or facilitate a reentry of older workers into the labor force.

Housing, or residential investment, has been mentioned as probably the single, most common investment of older people. About 70% of older people in the United States own their homes. It is dubious whether this statistic will hold up for future generations, given the present rate of inflation and escalating costs of housing. Inflation is a hidden form of taxation, and it certainly conspires against the accumulation of assets among young people. It may well be that we are seeing the last generation of home owners in such large proportions. But even for older persons, home-owning is in jeopardy. Utilities and home repairs take an exorbitant toll, even after taking into account property tax concessions. No wonder, then, that the Comprehensive Service amendments to the Older Americans Act of 1974 mandated home repair as a priority service.

There are some experiments of reverse mortgage (or, actually a positive mortgage system) which may be pointed to. It consists simply of a mechanism by which elderly home owners transfer their property after death to a community nonprofit corporation with the right to live in the home until death. In the meantime, the person begins collecting reverse mortgage— monthly payments for the home from the corporation that also takes over the maintenance and tax payments for that dwelling unit. Older people understand little about the meaning of this. It will take probably another generation to educate the public about the potential virtues of the reverse mortgage. Nearly 75% of all federal, state, and local expenditures for the elderly are going to income maintenance programs. Very little goes into services.

There are different policy interpretations for this. There is a theory that claims that these are different philosophies for different age groups. We relate to children and young adults with services, but we relate to older people with income transfers. We do not see the necessity of providing services to older persons because it does not enter the domain of our outlook or national character. To a certain extent, this theory is justified. Most services for older people are for catastrophic emergencies, and there are few preventive or supporting services. One of the reasons we do not have services is that we have never adopted (had the courage to adopt) a policy for extending life expectancy. In a political sense, it is very risky to say that everyone should live to age 100. There is no such explicit or even implicit policy objective. Consequently, there is ambivalence about services that are life-enhancing for older people. Life expectancy still increases because there are certain dynamics in technological societies that leads to such a demographic phenomenon; but this happens while services and income maintenance for older persons are problematic and controversial. We are still glamorizing youth and may still be at the point mentioned by Margaret Mead: In our society the old are strangers in the land of the young.

BIOLOGICAL
AND
PSYCHOLOGICAL
PERSPECTIVES

3

THE ISSUE OF BIOLOGICAL AND PSYCHOLOGICAL DEFICITS

Carl Eisdorfer and Donna Cohen

The purpose of this chapter is to stimulate discussion on a topic that has generated substantial controversy among gerontologists: In what sense is it meaningful to refer to biological and psychological deficits during adult development and aging? Our approach poses this question with reference to the theoretical assumptions, methodological tools, and empirical data preeminent in aging research (see Finch & Hayflick, 1977; Birren and Schaie, 1977; Binstock and Shanas, 1977). Our basic line of argument is simple, though it may take some time to develop: Our current knowledge does not allow us to tell with a high degree of accuracy what biological and psychological deficits occur as a function of aging.

The classification of deficits is a popular exercise in the literature on aging. This chapter will have served its purpose if it shows the reader the parameters of the "deficit" issue and provokes the initiation of new ways to identify and measure changes in the aging and aged.

49

AGE: A PROCESS WITH ANTECEDENTS

It is important to consider the ways in which age as a construct is used or misused. Aging evokes images, but one must appreciate that aging is more than an esthetic reference to the aged. Indeed, aging has only a limited relation to old people. Aging is a process. If the term "aging" is used descriptively, it refers to a sequence of changes across a lifespan. Of course, it is possible to isolate an interval in the lifespan from its antecedents, either physiologic, sociologic, or psychologic. It is impossible, however, to do so without risking some distortion. Statements about dimensions of change (e.g., cognition, personality, cerebral blood flow, or oxidative phosphorylation) at age 65 are inadequate without a developmental formulation which provides a context for understanding the change being described.

A second important consideration is the explanatory value of age. If we agree: (1) to identify and describe some specified behavioral or biological variables that may change; and (2) to consider antecedent and contextual factors thought to contribute to change, we must also specify a method for measuring the antecedent variables independently for the targeted behavioral or biologic changes. This enables us to examine the relevance of the method both to the variable being evaluated and the aged subject as well.

Aging should not be considered a sufficient explanation for change without supporting data. It is, for example, inappropriate to describe a series of physical and mental changes in an older individual and then conclude that "Mrs. X forgets things because she is old"; this is a conjectural statement and more accurately should be phrased: "Mrs. X forgets things" and independently unless the relationship is further substantiated: "Mrs. X is ____ years old."

Our challenge is to find methods to measure forgetting and aging independently. At this time, however, we must introduce the constructs of primary and secondary aging (Busse, 1969). It should be recognized that when we study older persons we are really observing the interaction of accumulated events. Some occur simply with the passage of time (i.e., primary aging). In addition, there are events such as disease and trauma, related to longevity, which occur randomly but accumulate with longer life; this phenomenon is referred to as secondary aging. Thus, when we examine changes in an older person, we are not simply measuring the effects of age per se, we are looking at age and age-disease interactions. Very simply, if you are 50 years old, you have had twice as great an opportunity as a twenty-five year old to have a variety of things happen to you (e.g., exposure to viruses, life stresses, mutagens, and so on).

RESEARCH STRATEGIES

This brings us back to the problem of deficits and to one of the issues in this chapter: To what extent do our research strategies permit us to attribute biological and psychosocial change to primary or secondary aging during adult development and aging? Our knowledge of aging is contaminated by the research strategies we use to find out what we think we know or believe we know. For example, early cross-sectional analyses of intellectual test scores and age indicated that most human abilities reached their peak between the late teens and midtwenties and then declined progressively thereafter (Wechsler, 1944). There are now data from a number of studies which question these conclusions (Eisdorfer, 1978; Jarvik et al., 1973), and the evidence suggests that there is no clear peaking of intelligence during the third decade of life. Data from the longitudinal Berkeley Growth Study (Eichorn, 1973) show an overall trend of an increase in performance scores from 16-36 years, although at a decelerating rate for men, while females show a very slight decline after 26 years. No single subtest,

however, conforms exactly to the pattern. Honzik and Mac-
Farland (1973) reported stable growth from 6-40 years. Even
Botwinick (1977), Horn (1975, 1977) and others who have been
major proponents of the hypothesis supporting an early decline in intelligence agree that there is no simple unidimen-
sional drop in intelligence. The issues in fact should not be so
much decline-versus-no-decline, but what, if any, components
change, when (rather than if), and under what conditions (if
any), is decline observed (Eisdorfer, 1978; Eichorn, 1973).

Although many of the cross-sectional studies on intelligence
and aging demonstrated a difference in performance in older
individuals relative to the young, it would be unfair to dismiss
them as false. Indeed the data themselves are probably correct.
What is important is to recognize that we made an error in
interpreting data, that is, in believing that a young cohort compared with an older cohort at a given point in time had predictive validity for the younger cohort. Cross-sectional designs
continue to be the predominant research strategy in aging, despite the empirical advantages of a longitudinal design. Our
choice of design, while in part a product of our scientific pro-
clivity, is as often influenced by such "external" criteria as
economics, convenience, and academic survival. In view of
such "practical" considerations, cross-sectional strategies
often emerge as the paradigm of choice.

Longitudinal strategies have increased our descriptive
power of cognitive development and change but not necessarily our explanatory power. In this context very few studies
have taken seriously the utility of primary and secondary aging
as constructs to explain change when it does occur.

A number of investigators (Jarvik, 1973; Savage et al., 1973)
have emphasized that in the absence of illness, cognitive stability is the rule even through the ninth decade. Wilkie and Eisdorfer (1971) are among the few investigators who specifically
measured a health variable in relation to cognitive change

occurring across time. They reported that elevated diastolic blood pressure rather than age per se was a factor in the intellectual decline of a group of subjects first seen at ages 60-69, and then followed over a ten-year-period using the WAIS. Subjects were drawn from the Duke Longitudinal Study and showed no decline at least through the eighth decade of life if they had normal or slightly elevated diastolic blood pressure. Those hypertensive subjects first seen between ages 70-79 did not survive the ten-year-follow-up.

Cross-sequential research designs are an effective compromise between cross-sectional and longitudinal strategies (Baltes et al., 1977). They have a format for gathering data relatively efficiently and also for minimizing the confounding cohort variable. Evidence for biologic and psychologic change resulting from even the best longitudinal research is contaminated by the occurrence in the history of the individual of specific historic events, and these cohort effects (e.g., education, nutrition, socioeconomic variables), are potent mediators of performance. Indeed, we are a long way from a full understanding of the impact of early environmental stimulation or of education at various points throughout the subsequent lifespan.

The importance of the cohort effect is illustrated by the significant increase in the prevalence of Parkinson's disease with advancing age followed by a fall over time in the prevalence of the disease. It was subsequently discovered that many people showing the symptoms were among those who had been infected in 1917-1921 with a viral flu strain causing central nervous system destruction (Duvoisin and Yahr, 1965; Duvoisin et al., 1963). Thus many people who were alive in the 1920s and were affected by the toxic virus lived long enough to display Parkinson's deficits in later life. For a time, clinicians and scientists were misled and mistakenly attributed the disease to aging.

THERAPEUTIC NIHILISM AND
PERSONAL EXPECTANCIES

Before reviewing the status of current theoretical and empirical systems in gerontology, it may be useful to examine an attitude that has prevailed about the inevitability of age. Nihilistic beliefs have flourished in public—as well as in scientific circles—proposing that aging brings universal, inevitable, and irreversible deficits in body and mind, despite the lack of empirical support for such conclusions. We believe that such a priori beliefs (and not data) have significantly retarded a constructive societal response to deal with significant change in the age structure of the world population (Butler, 1978; Eisdorfer, 1978; Maddox, 1978). It has also affected the support of data finding enterprises.

It is true that the process(es) of aging affects the ability of humans to adapt to their world in a number of profound ways. Bio-psychosocial changes throughout the lifespan significantly mediate the quality of life. Furthermore, demographic studies confirm the predictions of Gompertz' plot of mortality (Gompertz, 1825): the older the individual, the more likely he or she is to die. It is also clear that the older person has an increased risk for most diseases, and that 75-80% of all persons 65 years and older have at least one chronic disease. It is perhaps of greater significance that 47% of older Americans report some limitation in their daily activities (DHEW, 1978).

It might be worth speculating that the current prevalence of illness among the aged is a cohort effect that will change as the younger generations grow older. But the prevalence of certain diseases such as depression (Gurland, 1976) and dementing illness (Gruenberg, 1978) portend a particularly bleak future. For example, demographic projections show that the portion of the aged in our society is increasing (Hauser, 1973); the epidemiologic data clearly indicate that the risk to cognitive disease increases geometrically after age 60 (Kay, 1977; Goldman, 1978); and our rehabilitation and treatment strategies are extremely limited (Eisdorfer et al., forthcoming).

The facts we have presented concern illness, disease, and a range of chronic disabilities readily apparent in the frail elderly. Indeed, disease, rather than health, has been the focus for much of the social and health services developed for the aged. We appear to have ignored the potential for creating programs that maximize opportunities for the older person, that maintain skills, and promote health and well-being throughout the lifespan.

The therapeutic nihilism of many health professionals toward older people is only one reflection of our society's resistance to care for the aged—a sharp contrast to our values for infants and children. Older persons arc often seen as generally undesirable patients and unappealing persons. The lack of investment in such patients, the attitude that the older person is no longer useful in society, and the perceived psychosocial changes in the older individual's lifespace (loneliness, isolation, existential sadness, and so forth), generate an additional set of problems in clinical caring for the aged.

Little is done, by way of governmentally sponsored programs, to help older people with health maintenance through periodic health examinations, continued education, or the opportunity to work productively. Federal and state intervention have been heavily invested in hospital and nursing-home care, and economic, housing, social services, or family support have not been used to maintain a person at home in lieu of institutionalization, rhetoric not withstanding (Eisdorfer et al., forthcoming). Twenty-five years ago the aged (65 years and older) received 2% of outpatient mental health care, although they made up more than 25% of all state hospital admissions. Today the aged still receive only 2% of outpatient care, but instead of being admitted to state hospitals for cognitive and emotional disorders, they are entered in nursing homes (Kramer et al., 1973). Many of these nursing homes may be described as ministate hospitals without benefit of the appropriate staff.

Nursing-home care is confusing and signals our continued nihilistic posture toward the aged. Although such institutions represent at least potentially a health resource, nursing-home facilities have been largely disconnected from the health care system and its educational base. In addition, as we indicated earlier, current federal reimbursement schedules for long-term care have hindered the development of appropriate resources in the community as alternatives to institutional care. The paucity of professionals trained to work in long-term care and low state payments under Medicaid (which contribute to remarkable levels of staff turnover), and the use of nursing homes as custodial rather than therapeutic alternatives to state hospitals, have further contributed to pessimism concerning the aged (Eisdorfer et al., forthcoming).

The attitude of the aged toward personal health is an additional major obstacle. In the Duke Longitudinal Study, 44% of those in poor health, as assessed in a medical evaluation, rated themselves in good or excellent condition (Busse, 1969). Other barriers involve the failure of older persons to trust physicians (particularly young physicians), the fear of hospitals as a place to die, a tendency to self-medicate, and the failure to understand or follow instructions—all of which exacerbate the problem. The point is that the subjective appraisal of aging and health among the elderly themselves is complicated. If the aged regard themselves as old, then they tend to accept infirmity as part of their old age. Likewise, physicians see older people as more likely to be disabled or sick and therefore regard illness of the aged as acceptable since it is "normal." In both instances there is a reason for questioning these premises. A major educational program is mandatory not only for health care professionals but also for the aging and the aged.

In summary, personal expectancies or personal assumptions are contaminating factors in any evaluation of biological and psychological changes with aging. One's ability to learn, assumptions about one's capacity for making contributions to society, and untested assumptions about a restricted array of disabilities, determine what people say and how they perform. Indeed, artificial deficits may be created through what might be called self-labeling.

AGING: AN ECLECTIC SCIENCE

Not only does aging have a brief empirical history, but we have also looked at it through the blinders of our special disciplines. Our specific interests as scientists and scholars have clearly distorted the process of aging we measure and describe. Very simply, if we use a magnifying glass, a microscope, or a psychological interview to examine aging in a tissue or behavior, we have a high probability of distorting the significance of a single line of biological or psychological observation. Variables such as neurofibrillary tangles, memory dysfunction, loss of energy, or atherosclerosis plaques, become associated with the process of aging rather than the pathology.

Aging is difficult to define empirically because the level of analysis varies across a spectrum of molecular, cellular, tissue, organ, and system changes. Therefore, unless one has the memory capacity of a high speed computer or an accomplished cohort of distinguished colleagues, comprehending the literature on aging has all the architectural mystery of a Japanese garden, where one moves from one stepping stone to another. An example is the documented loss of neurons in the central nervous system (Brody and Vijayashankar, 1976). There is a considerable body of data indicating that neurons are lost and that among cortical neurons, dendrites are lost (Scheibel and Scheibel, 1975). The attention devoted to this finding has not, however, been extended to determining what relations exist between such loss and performance. The simplistic notion of a

1:1 correspondence between anatomic loss and ability has led to the assumption that brain size predicts the level of intelligence. We know that this is false, yet we have believed that computerized axial tomograph (CAT) scans of the cranial cavity could predict extent of dementia. Only now do we have evidence that this may not be true and that behavioral indices are important for the diagnosis of dementing illness (Nathan, 1978). This is not a vindication of behavioral over biological variables, but merely a comment on the tendency to confuse the output of expensive technology with fact and counting the numerical output without understanding the relation in question. While mathematics is the language of science, irrelevant numbers are no substitute for establishing the factual nature of the relation between empirical variables.

TECHNOLOGY: MEASURES AND MEANING

As described earlier, one of the most influential concepts to result from years of research is that elemental structural change does not imply a corresponding functional change. For example, we use a cryomicrotome to slice a small piece of the brain tissue and then proceed to stain and count neurons, dendritic spines, plaques, neurofibrillary tangles, and so on. We also have developed the technology to measure the concentration and activities of the brain's neurotransmitters (Finch, 1977; Horita, 1978). But what do histological and neurochemical observations say about cognitive capacity and adaptive behavior? A more productive way to phrase the question may be to ask: What are the different anatomic observations we might count, what is their regional variation, and how do they relate to changes in neurotransmitters and their enzymes? Finally, what precise behavioral alterations can we attribute to such change? It is naïve to think that a change in cognition involves change in a single neuronal system or neurotransmitter, but as our neurochemical analyses improve, we should be able to understand the complex arrangements of neuronal and glial systems in the aging brain as well as the balance of many neurotransmitter systems in conjunction with behavior.

Technological developments often create more questions than answers. For instance, CT is a relatively new method for visualizing brain structures (New and Scott, 1975). In this procedure, a rotating X-ray source with detector crystals takes thousands of pinpoint readings which are processed by computers. The computer readings are then converted to pictures showing different sections of the brain where brightness is proportional to the absorption coefficient of the corresponding area of the brain. Because CT provides a safe and accurate visualization of cerebral structures it has become an invaluable tool in the evaluation of irreversible dementing illness, specifically the identification of mass lesions or hydrocephalic conditions. A characteristic feature of Alzheimer's disease, the most common form of the dementia, is gross atrophy of the brain, widening of the cortical sulci, and enlargement of the ventricles. Cortical and central atrophy, however, are also seen in CT scans of normal elderly people (Barron et al., 1976; Glydensted, 1977; Wu, 1978). Perhaps with advancing CT technology (e.g., "region of interest" intensification measures) parameters reflecting the effectiveness of brain-behavior relations may be defined.

One additional point merits attention. In the history of science, technological developments in specific disciplines have often opened the way to understand the finer structure of molecules, cells, tissues, and organ systems. In each instance, after a flurry of enthusiasm, we learned that knowledge brings the recognition that new questions need to be addressed. The complexity of human behavior; the interrelation of cognitive, motivational, and response-producing processes; and the measurement of changes during development and aging, defies easy solution and may require simultaneous technical and conceptual breakthroughs in several disciplines.

DEFICIT OR CHANGE?

The term "deficit" has been used at least three ways in the field of aging: (1) as a nihilistic metaphor; (2) as a description of age change in behavior; and (3) as an explanation of age-related changes in behavior. But a metaphor is hardly an hypothesis or an empirical entity, and a behavioral description is not an explanation. For example, the data indicate that, at least through age 75, behavioral changes may be as related to physical and environmental problems as they are to age changes in the body machinery per se. When behavior is impaired, the etiology should be identified and clarified through a careful investigation. A host of variables affect performance change, including sensory acuity, experience and training, self-esteem, competence, environmental supports, motivation, health, integrity of the immune and central nervous systems, as well as the expectancies of the subject and experimenter for success. Indeed, the analysis of change requires measurement of multiple, concurrent physiological, behavioral, psychosocial, and environmental factors.

Although this is not the place to analyze the difficult problem of measuring change in detail, it is appropriate to at least summarize some of the beliefs held by gerontologists. There are distinct motivational factors that affect the response production of older persons in test situations. Cautiousness, fear of failure, and withholding responses, are among the characteristics observed in the older adult which may be incorrectly interpreted as "deficit" behavior. These changes in cognitive style could also be regarded as part of an adaptive response repertoire which reflect a potential change in the motivation or experience of the older person. Artificial test situations and rewards meaningful to a younger population may have less value for the old, and therefore tend to produce less productive, efficient behavior. Sensory acuity does decline in older adults, but it is a mistake to surmise that perceptual, attentional, and memory mechanisms may likewise deteriorate in a one-to-one ratio. Development is more than adding new skills and subtracting them incrementally, but also involves the organization of abilities. Therefore, it may be unreasonable to assume that changes with aging should be analyzed as simple increases or losses or even as curvilinear change. It is also not appropriate to assume that older persons will exhibit deteriorating cognitive and personality functioning as part of normal aging (during which numerous biological changes occur).

If the notion of deficit as an explanatory variable is to be disregarded, how can we formulate an alternative strategy for the study and explanation of alterations of behavior in persons of any age? We suggest that a series of testable questions need to be formulated to evaluate the interaction between the process, the person, and the situation. For example: (1) How does the older individual perceive the environment? (2) How is the knowledge of the environment represented in the brain? (3) What is the motive of the individual and how does it influence how the older individual perceives, remembers, and responds to environmental cues? (4) How do physical factors affect the way the older individual performs? (5) How do these change over time?

These questions, hardly meant to be inclusive, provide one framework to analyze the adaptation of the individual to his or her environment. Another set of questions can be formulated to evaluate the relation between central nervous system alterations and behavior: What biological changes in the nervous, endocrine, and immune systems are causal in age-related or pathology related changes? (Jarvik and Cohen, 1973; Cohen, forthcoming). For example, recent data demonstrate that plasma norepinephrine levels are significantly greater in the early evening in older persons, and, further, that this nighttime effect is correlated with poor sleeping patterns. Since plasma norepinephrine levels are thought to reflect sympathetic nervous system activity, and since the latter is accompanied by a more aroused physiological state, it may be that significant nighttime sympathetic activity interferes with sleep in certain individuals, for example, the elderly (Prinz et al., 1978). And sleep patterns may mediate behavior. Can we safely intervene to alter *catecholamine* levels, sleep patterns, and behavior, or, alternately, locate subjects in whom levels vary and then measure behavior? Albeit somewhat reductionistic, this strategy takes us from age related behavioral defects to an understanding of a mechanism. Similarly, psychological changes of one type could be an etiological factor reflected in measured changes of a different sort (e.g., anxiety in relation to a test situation could result in performance deficit seen in turn as a learning defect).

A number of relevant variables have implications for human adaptation with aging—health, social interaction, ability to work, finances, self-esteem, and so on (Eisdorfer, 1972). Personal adjustments which occur during life transitions such as retirement are better analyzed as adaptive (or nonadaptive) role changes. The concept of deficit has little meaning, independent of an accompanying idea of to what it is to be adapted. In this vein, many tests of ability are irrelevant to the aged since they derive conceptually from measures and adaptation to situations, largely irrelevant for the aged (e.g., school performance). Thompson and Streib (1958) demonstrated, and others have duplicated (Martin and Doron, 1966; Ryser and Sheldon, 1969) the finding that poor health is a frequent antecedent to retirement, and an improvement in health rather than poorer health is seen in many persons immediately after retirement.

The effect of interpersonal loss (including job or the death of spouse or friends) is another extremely important explanatory concept needed to understand the behavior of aging persons. However, losses in the social support network may reveal little about adaptation without some knowledge of either the intensity or desirability of lost jobs, friends, and activities. Furthermore, data describing the social contacts and the social interactions of the aged should also be interpreted in the context of the economics of social participation (Rosow, 1967; Eisdorfer, 1972). Although the statement that "money is critical to adaptation" is hardly profound, there have been few studies evaluating the psychological, social, cultural, and economic aspects of income restrictions after retirement. An interesting observation was made by Neugarten who pointed out that on-time (expected) versus off-time (unanticipated) losses may have quite different consequences. There are a number of social-psychological mediators which diminish the stressful impact of an on-time loss such as widowhood in the older, as compared to the younger, individual (Eisdorfer and Wilkie, 1977).

Before concluding this section, it is worthwhile to review an important scientific principle to facilitate our understanding of adaptation and change. Data collection and analysis should be done in a way that tests a specific hypothesis, or the explanatory power, of a theory. Eisdorfer (1972) evaluated the differential ability of a crisis model versus a reinforcement model versus a motivational model to organize a series of observations to understand the adjustment to retirement. Although each model was able to describe and predict individual adaptation to a limited degree, sustained research would be necessary to empirically establish which one (or combination) best accounted for adaptation to retirement. Perhaps the most interesting conclusion of all was that variations in socioeconomic status, and in the time pre- and postretirement at which measurements were made, was most predictive of all. This emphasizes a significant observation in the field of aging —the high variability among the aged, and the importance of time sampling in relation to critical events.

SELECTIVE AGING

Selective survival is a significant antecedent condition that may distort our understanding of any changes reported in an

aging population. In different parts of the world, individuals
survive as a function of those specific bio-psychosocial factors
which pay off in that environment. Thus, the aged are a pre-
selected group of survivors in a given setting. For example,
sickle cell anemia, which is generally transmitted among
blacks, appears to have been at least somewhat adaptive for
people living in certain geographical regions by protecting the
carrier from malaria. But it significantly compromises the
ability of afflicted individuals to survive in high altitudes at
lower air pressures.

Lifestyle as well as genetics can be a significant determinant
of disease status in middle and late life. Friedman and Roseman
have described their investigations of the coronary prone behavior pattern among middle-aged men (Roseman, 1974).
Although Type A constellation of behavior characterized by
an extreme obsession with time, explosiveness of speech, and
excess competition, has not been investigated developmen-
tally, there does not appear to be much evidence for the predictive utility of Type A behavior and heart disease in older people
(Cohen, 1977a,b). It may be that Type A individuals who enjoy
such a lifestyle will live longer. Alternatively, those in whom
Type A and some other biological factors interact to produce
an individual prone to myocardial-infarction (MI), die young;
or the experience of an MI in an individual with a biological
susceptibility to the traumatic effects of Type A behavior is
traumatized enough to cause him to change from the Type A
lifestyle. In any case, the association of behavioral dimensions with morbidity and mortality are important relations
that remain to be examined in prospective longitudinal studies.

Personality changes in both intrapsychic and psychosocial
adaptation have been reported in men and women in their
forties (Neugarten et al., 1964; Neugarten and Gutman, 1968;
Lowenthal et al., 1975). Women tend to become more expressive and aggressive, whereas older men become more passive
and nurturant. Cohen (1977) demonstrated that self-ratings

of overt measures of personality confirmed the findings of internal personality measures (Neugarten, 1968, 1973). This change in roles should hardly be construed as a deficit.

A deficit may, however, be redefined as the result of what society chooses to use or not use, believe or not believe. Indeed, in some primitive cultures (Amoss and Harrell, forthcoming), older women become very powerful witches and older men loveable storytellers. It is important to emphasize that sex differences are a significant, recurrent observation throughout development and aging (Cohen and Wilkie, 1978). Lowenthal and her colleagues (1975) reported that sex differences were generally larger than life-style differences in their study of life-span transitions. She stressed that the difference between men and women must be understood in terms of developmental shifts in needs, goals, and expectations. It is also well-known that women live longer than men and do not have the same risk of disease and illness. A variety of biological and psychosocial hypotheses have been advanced to account for this selective survival and mortality. Furthermore, sex differences are only one aspect of a larger consideration—the explanation of individual differences during aging.

CONCLUSION

Our brief consideration of lifespan change and adaptation leads us to conclude with two final observations. Our society has not clearly defined its expectations for adjustment, including social roles, for the aging and aged. By contrast, older macaque (monkey) females play crucial social roles by posting the boundaries of the group and protecting the babies from younger aggressive males searching for a weaker animal to test their assertiveness and strength. Other nonhuman primates who travel in packs, with the older animals outside, move to the signal of the old leader. At least in nonhuman primates there appears to exist a perception of the assets, wisdom, and understanding of the older animals. It could be argued that the older monkeys are on the periphery of the pack because they are the most expendable. Indeed, we are presented with an interesting social tradeoff which should not be taken lightly in the development of any social policy.

It is clearly inappropriate to amputate the aged from our society and clearly appropriate that we develop positive social roles (even if the positive social roles of the aged are necessary to protect the rest of personkind from being eliminated!). The changing age structure of the world poses a serious, longterm dilemma requiring a societal response. There should be little question in the reader's mind that we make social policy by passive response and belief systems more often than on data. Our plea is that we recognize these shortcomings. It is often just as bitter a fate to construct social policy from poor data as from no data, and indeed the knowledge of one's ignorance is far more enlightening than the assured posture of the faithful believer of false information.

Gerontology is an interdisciplinary field and truly a science in its infancy. It has grown from a tradition in which clinical and basic scientific investigators added an age variable to whatever investigation they were conducting in their respective disciplines. In the past few decades aging has become a concern of both multidisciplinary and interdisciplinary research and planning, and we have begun to accrue data on aging in the psychological, biological, and social sciences. Indeed, the National Institute of Aging was only established in 1976, and is the youngest of all the Institutes of the N.I.H. Our society is just beginning to address and deal with the issues of aging, not only as a part of a national social welfare policy, but also to develop the knowledge to support, direct, and adjust our policies (Busse, 1978).

REFERENCES

BALTES, P. B., H. W. REESE, and J. R. NESSELROADE (1977) Life-Span Developmental Psychology: Introduction to Research Methods. Monterey, CA: Brooks/Cole.

BARRON, S., L. JACOBS, and W. KINKEL (1976) "Changes in size of normal lateral ventricles during aging determined by computerized tomography." Neurology 26: 1011-1013.

BINSTOCK, R. and E. SHANAS (1977) Handbook of Aging and the Social Sciences. New York: Van Nostrand Reinhold.

BIRREN, J. E. and K. W. SCHAIE [eds.] (1977) Handbook of the Psychology of Aging. New York: Van Nostrand Reinhold.

BOTWINICK, J. (1977) "Intellectual abilities," in J. E. Birren and K. W. Schaie (eds.) Handbook of the Psychology of Aging. New York; Van Nostrand Reinhold.

BRODY, H. and N. VIJAYASHANKAR (1977) "Anatomical changes in the nervous system," in C. Finch and L. Hayflick (eds.) Handbook of the Biology of Aging. New York: Van Nostrand Reinhold.

BUSSE, E. W. (1978) "Aging research: a review and critique," in G. Usdin and C. J. Hofling (eds.) Aging: The Process and the People. New York: Brunner/Mazel.

——— (1969) "Theories of aging," in E. W. Busse and E. Pfeiffer (eds.) Behavior and Adaption in Later Life. Boston: Little, Brown.

——— (1967) "Changes in thinking and behavior in the elderly: an interdisciplinary study." Presented at the annual meeting of the American Psychiatric Association, May, Detroit.

BUTLER, R. (1978) "National Institute of Mental Health Study," in R. Katzman, R. Terry, and K. Bick (eds.) Alzheimer's Disease: Senile Dementia and Related Disorders. New York: Raven.

COHEN, D. (forthcoming) "Biobehavioral models of cognitive dysfunction in the aged," in R. Sprott (ed.) Aging and Intellectual Change. New York: Van Nostrand Reinhold.

——— (1977a) "Cardiovascular disease history and behavior patterns." Perceptual Motor Skills 44: 152-154.

——— (1977b) "Sex differences in overt personality patterns in older men and women." Gerontology 23: 262-266.

——— and D. WILKIE (forthcoming) "Sex differences in cognition in the elderly," in M. Wittig and D. Peterson (eds.) Determinants of Sex-Related Differences in Cognitive Functioning. New York: Academic Press.

DUVOISIN, R. C. and M. D. YAHR (1963) "Encephalitis and Parkinsonism." Archives of Neurology 12: 227-239.

——— M. D. SCHWEITZER, and H. A. MERRIT (1963) "Parkinsonism before and since the epidemic of encephalitis lethargica." Archives of Neurology 9: 38-42.

EICHORN, D. H. (1973) "The Institute of Human Development Studies, Berkeley and Oakland," in C. F. Jarvik, J. E. Blum, and C. Eisdorfer (eds.) Intellectual Functioning in Adults. New York: Springer Verlag.

EISDORFER, C. (forthcoming) "Afterword: the implications for public policy of other ways of growing old," in P. Amos and S. Harrel (eds.) Other Ways of Growing Old. Palo Alto: Stanford University Press.

———— (1978a) "Psychophysiologic and cognitive studies in the aged," in G. Usdin and C. K. Hofling (eds.) Aging: The Process and the People. New York: Bruner/ Mazel.

———— (1978b) "Societal response to aging: some possible consequences," in L. F. Jarvik (ed.) Aging into the 21st Century. New York: Gardner Press.

———— (1972) "Adaption to loss of work," in F. Carp (ed.) Retirement. New York: Behavioral Publications.

———— and D. COHEN (forthcoming) "The assessment of organic impairment in the aged: in search of a new mental status examination," in E. Burdock, Sudilovsky, and S. Gershon (eds.) Quantitative Techniques for the Evaluation of Psychiatric Patients. New York: Marcel Dekker.

———— (1978) "The cognitively impaired elderly: differential diagnoses," in M. Storandt, I. C. Siegler, and M. F. Elias (eds.) The Clinical Psychology of Aging. New York: Plenum.

———— and C. PRESTON (forthcoming) "Behavioral and psychological therapies for the older patient with cognitive impairment," in G. Cohen and N. Miller (eds.) Behavioral Aspects of Senile Dementia. New York: Raven.

EISDORFER, C. and F. WILKIE (1977) "Stress, disease, aging, and behavior," in J. E. Birren and K. W. Schaie (eds.) Handbook of the Psychology of Aging. New York: Van Nostrand Reinhold.

FINCH, C. E. (1977) "Neuroendocrine and autonomic aspects of aging," in C. Finch and L. Hayflick (eds.) Handbook of the Biology of Aging. New York: Van Nostrand Reinhold.

———— and L. HAYFLICK [eds.] (1977) Handbook of the Biology of Aging. New York: Van Nostrand Reinhold.

GLYDENSTED, C. (1977) "Measurements of the normal ventricular system and hemispheric sulci of 100 adults with comute tomography." Neuroradiology 14: 183-192.

GOLDMAN, R. (1978) "The social impact of the organic dementia of the aged," in K. Nandy (ed.) Senile Dementia: A Biomedical Approach. New York: Elsevier/ North.

GOMPERTZ, B. (1825) "On the nature of the function expressive of the law of human mortality and on a new mode of determining life contingencies." Philosophical Transactions of the Royal Society (London) 115: 513-585.

GRUENBERG, E. (1978) "Epidemiology," in R. Datzman, R. Terry, and K. Bick (eds.) Alzheimer's Disease: Senile Dementia and Related Disorders. New York: Raven.

GURLAND, B. J. (1976) "The comparative frequency of depression in various adult age groups." Journal of Gerontology 31: 283-292.

HAUSER, P. M. (1977) "Aging and world-wide population change," in R. H. Binstock and E. Shanas (eds.) Handbook of Aging and the Social Sciences. New York: Van Nostrand Reinhold.

HONZIK, M. P. and J. W. MacFARLANE (1973) "Personality development and intellectual functioning from 21 months to 40 years," in L. F. Jarvik, J. E. Blum, and C. Eisdorfer (eds.) Intellectual Functioning in Adults. New York: Springer Verlag.

HORITA, A. (1978) "Neuropharmacology and aging," in J. Roberts, R. Adelman, and V. Cristofalo (eds.) Pharmacological Intervention in the Aging Process. New York: Plenum.

HORN, J. (1977) "Nuances of intellectual development." Presented at the Conference of Cognition and Aging, Seattle, January.

HORN, J. L. (1975) "Psychometric studies of aging and intelligence," in S. Gershon and A. Raskin (eds.) Genesis and Treatment of Psychologic Disorders in the Elderly. New York: Raven.

JARVIK, C. F. (1973) "Discussion," in C. F. Jarvik, J. E. Blum, and C. Eisdorfer (eds.) Intellectual Functioning in Adults. New York: Springer Verlag.

——— and D. COHEN (1973) "A Biological approach to intellectual changes with aging," in C. Eisdorfer and M. P. Lawton (eds.) The Psychology of Adult Development in Aging. Washington, DC: American Psychological Association.

JARVIK, C. F., J. E. BLUM, and C. EISDORFER (eds.) (1973) Intellectual Functioning in Adults. New York: Springer Verlag.

KAY, D.W.K. (1977) "The epidemiology of brain deficit in the aged: problems in patient identification," in C. Eisdorfer and R. O. Friedel (eds.) Cognitive and Emotional Disturbances in the Elderly. Washington, DC: American Psychological Association.

KRAMER, M., C. A. TAUBE, and R. W. REDICK (1973) "Patterns of psychiatric facilities in the aged: past, present, and future," in C. Eisdorfer and M. P. Lawton (eds.) The Psychology of Adult Development and Aging. Washington, DC: American Psychological Association.

LOWENTHAL, M. F., M. THURNHER, and D. CHIRIBOGA [eds.] (1975) Four Stages of Life. San Francisco: Jossey-Bass.

MADDOX, G. L. (1978) "The social and cultural context of aging," in G. Usdin and C. J. Hofling (eds.) Aging: The Process and the People. New York: Brunner/Mazel.

NATHAN, R. J. (1978) "Cerebral atrophy and independence in the elderly." Presented at the annual meeting of the American Psychiatric Association, Atlanta, May.

NEUGARTEN, B. L. (1974) "Adult personality: toward a psychology of the life cycle," in B. L. Neugarten (ed.) Middle Age and Aging. Chicago: University of Chicago Press.

——— (1973) "Personality change in late life: a developmental perspective," in C. Eisdorfer and M. P. Lawton (eds.) Adult Development and Aging. Washington: American Psychological Association.

——— and D. GUTTMAN (1968) "Age-sex roles and personality in middle age: a thematic apperception study," in B. L. Neugarten (ed.) Middle Age and Aging. Chicago: University of Chicago Press.

NEUGARTEN, B. L. et al. (1964) Personality in Middle and Late Life. New York: Atherton.

NEW, F. and W. SCOTT (1975) Computerized Tomography of the Brain and Orbit. (EMI Scanning). Baltimore: Williams & Wilkins.

RASKIND, M., P. PRINZ, and J. HALTER (1979) "Diurnal variation of plasma catecholamines in men: relation to age and sleep pattern." Gerontologist 11: 134.

ROSENMAN, R. (1974) "The role of behavior patterns and neurogenic factors in pathogenesis of coronary heart disease," in R. S. Elliot (ed.) Stress and the Heart. New York: Futura.

ROŞOW, I. (1967) Social Integration of the Aged. New York: Free Press.

RYSER, C., and A. SHELDON (1967) "Retirement and health." Journal of American Geriatric Association 17: 180-190.

SAVAGE, R. D., P. G. BRITTON, N. BOLTON, AND E. H. HALL (1975) Intellectual Functioning in the Aged. New York: Barnes & Noble.

SCHEIBEL, M. E. and A. B. SCHEIBEL (1975) "Structured changes in the aging brain," in H. Brody, D. Harmon, and J. M. Ordy (eds.) Aging, Volume 1. New York: Raven.

THOMPSON, W. E., and G. F. STREIB (1958) "Situational determinants: Health and economic deprivation in retirement." Journal of Social Issues 14: 18-34.

WECHSLER, D. (1958) The Measurement of Adult Intelligence. Baltimore: Williams & Wilkins.

WELLS, C. E. (1978) "Chronic brain disease: an overview." American Journal of Psychiatry 135: 1-2.

WILKIE, F. and C. EISDORFER (1971) "Intelligence and blood pressure in the aged." Science 172: 959-962.

WU, S. (1978) "Cognitive correlate of computerized axial tomographic measures of diffuse cerebral atrophy." Ph.D. dissertation, University of Utah.

4

BIOLOGICAL AND PSYCHOLOGICAL FACTORS IN AGING

Raymond Harris

Certainly one of the most important issues confronting geriatrics and gerontology today is how to bring the medical profession more fully into the fold of geriatrics and gerontology. We all recognize the sensitive and inadequate relationship that now exists between the academic and medical professions. More physicians must be motivated to become more familiar with the increasingly important data in geriatrics and geronotology generated by research. More research, like that by Eisdorfer and Cohen in this volume, is necessary to interest more physicians in the problems of older people and to promote better interdisciplinary training in geriatrics for professional practitioners and paraprofessional workers in hospitals, social agencies, skilled nursing homes, and other health-related and community facilities. The lack of such training has led to ineffective treatment of elderly patients, the waste of large amounts of money, and staggering costs of health services for the aged—estimated at almost $41 billion.

It is essential to develop extensive interdisciplinary core curricula for geriatric training that improve: (1) the diagnosis, treatment, understanding, and care of the aging; (2) the ability to identify and assess the severity of important disease categories and age-associated conditions, and to make appropriate referrals; (3) the skills and competency in interpersonal relationships and the integration of human and community services; (4) professional-patient relationships; (5) the educational environment in schools, community organizations, institutions, and nursing homes. As Malcolm Knowles has emphasized, such educational programs should teach, by precept and example: (1) respect for personality; (2) participation in decision-making; (3) freedom of expression and the availability and exchange of information; and (4) mutuality of responsibility in defining and evaluating goals, planning, and activities.

The information most useful to health professionals in geriatrics and gerontology must be based on good data obtained from well-designed research. With its fundamental analysis of the problems inherent in research on aging, this article may shock the unwary or inexperienced researcher or practitioner in gerontology and geriatrics, for it points out that much data in the current literature on aging are contaminated by poor research strategies and designs, especially in the social and psychological sciences, but not necessarily confined to them.

In the future, any valid psychological research on aging, involving cognitive and intellectual functions, will require the investigator to know, either before or after testing, the biological strata and function of the brain. Researchers will need to obtain appropriate data from postmortem examinations or from noninvasive studies of brain function using modern technology. No longer can a researcher accept as a normal subject one who has not had a normal electroencephalogram, brain scan, echoencephalogram, and even a

CAT (computerized axial tomography) brain scan. Without such baseline data to detect subclinical disease of the brain, psychological data from older people cannot be attributed to aging, at least beyond a doubt, regardless of what cohort design is devised and followed. The absence of clinical illness is no longer sufficient to rule out subclinical disease that may skew the collection of psychological and other research data.

This lesson was dramatically driven home to me recently when a 68-year-old patient of mine died suddenly. His family, friends, and I regarded him as a man of normal intelligence. Certainly, he could have been included as a normal subject in almost any study of cognitive, intellectual and psychological functions. But at postmortem, it was found that his brain was riddled with widespread plaques of Alzheimer's disease which had not yet produced clinical evidence of dementia.

Certainly there is a great need to test by comprehensive and formal psychological procedures normal and nondemented subjects showing various degrees of intellectual deterioration. It is necessary to obtain postmortem examination in at least a small group of these patients to determine what correlations, if any, exist between the changes found in nondemented, clinically normal cases, and those mild but common features of declining intellectual function which are regarded as normal in middle and late life (Tomlinson et al., 1970). Such postmortem data would help to establish an epidemiological base that could be used statistically to determine the prevalence of subclinical disease in general aging populations and to validate the noninvasive tests of brain function and reduce the necessity for in-depth individual studies in every psychological research investigation.

Another stimulating question that comes to mind after reading Eisdorfer and Cohen's chapter is the question of when aging starts. In discussing the methodological problems of research, the authors appear to overlook this important question in biological research. Although many consider aging to be a universal attribute of life, qualified investigators in biology have maintained that aging begins when growth and development stop. For example, to obtain valid data on aging of the cardiovascular system, investigators, by modern standards, must be certain that they are actually studying biological aging (those changes which occur after the organism reaches adulthood), rather than the changes due to ordinary human growth and development during early years. One must compare the cardiovascular system of senile organisms with those of fully grown adults rather than with those of newborn or young organisms (Harris, 1979). Otherwise, the comparison would reflect the changes of growth and development rather than of aging. One could therefore ask if psychological data on aging in old people should not be compared with data from cohorts of mature subjects rather than from cohorts of younger subjects.

Another interesting point is that intellectual stimulation of the group must be taken into account in studies of psychological testing. It is possible that older people who continue to exercise their brain and grow mentally actually delay or reverse their psychological aging. There is an interesting analogy in biology. Biologists have long suspected that senescence may not affect some cold-blooded fish and reptiles which have indeterminate body sizes. Such animals, which grow as long as they live, may live as long as they grow (Goss, 1974). The kidneys and hearts of such fish and reptiles continue to produce new nephrons and muscle fibers throughout life, probably offsetting any loss of functional units. If this biological observation is correct, and animals do not age as long as they continue to grow, is it possible that this effect may potentially operate in the mental and psychological realm of aging people?

Could this growth effect also affect Erikson's "Epigenesis of a Life Cycle?" Erikson theorizes that at each age of life a new strength is added to a widening ensemble and reintegrated at each later stage to play its part in a full circle. In his opinion, any acute life crisis also arouses new energy in the patient. He believes it is questionable, however, if this occurs in old age when time is too short for alternate roads to integrity. As a result, Erikson believes that it is difficult for the older person to learn to mourn, to express grief and even rage and frustration since the older person is emotionally less elastic.

But what will be the effect of a longer life on the psychological changes of aging, especially in women whose average life expectancy between the years 1976 and 2050 will increase from 77 to 81 years? Will this longer life permit the aging person to follow alternate roads to psychological integrity and to repair their biological and psychological deficits as Erikson describes in younger people? Will appropriate therapy based on research data to meet the biological and psychological deficits enable elderly people to live longer and in better mental health?

The authors indicate that the term "deficit" is used in at least three ways in the field of aging: (1) as a nihilistic metaphor; (2) as a description of age change and behavior; (3) as an indication of age-related changes and behavior. This contention appears to substitute the biological and psychological deficits as metaphorical and semantical alternatives for the psychological changes of aging in our present state of research. Is it valid to consider the changes of aging as deficits when they may be normal for older people? If they are deficits (defined in the Webster dictionary as "a deficiency in amount or quality"), then compared to what are they deficits? What would happen if, instead of measuring deficits, we measured assets and called this chapter "The Issue of Biological and Psychological Assets in the Aged?" If we measure the assets of the elderly rather than their deficits, would the issues concerning research discussed in this paper be similar or different?

Finally, as a practicing physician, I agree with the importance of research in and for health maintenance and therapy of older people. Good research will enable more professional and paraprofessional practitioners in geriatrics and gerontology to develop and promote reasonable therapeutic expectations and sound objectives for older people who not only bear the crosses of age and diseases, but also face age-related economic, social, and cultural problems.

What are reasonable research expectations and sound objectives? More than 2400 years ago, Pindar, the ancient Greek poet, provided good advice when he wrote: "Do not yearn after immortality. But exhaust the limits of the possible!" We would do well to follow his advice.

REFERENCES

GOSS, R. J. (1974) "Aging versus growth." Perspectives of Biological Medicine (Summer): 485-494.
HARRIS, R. (1979) Aging of the Cardiovascular System. (Forthcoming)
TOMLINSON, B. E., G. BLESSED, and M. ROTH (1970) "Observation on the brains of demented old people." Journal of Neurological Science 11: 205-242.

HEALTH
AND
WELFARE
PERSPECTIVES

5

RESEARCH PATTERNS IN THE HEALTH OF THE ELDERLY: THE COMMUNITY MENTAL HEALTH CENTER

Eugene Litwak

The following areas of research are the principal burden of this chapter: first, the "natural" systems that support elderly in the community and that in turn make the concept of a community mental health center a real one; second, the organization of community mental health centers that permit them to reach selected groups of people in need of help as well as coordinate their services with other agencies in the community. An assessment of the general mental health problems of the aged and those which are currently serviced by community mental health centers will be discussed. The chapter will conclude with some comments on the need for better methods for implementing the laws of evaluation in centers so that meaningful evaluation information can be produced and utilized, and the

AUTHOR'S NOTE: An earlier version of this chapter was prepared for the Conference on Service Issues in Mental Health Aging, June 1976, Bethesda, MD.

need for developing standardized instruments to measure mental health problems at various levels.

NATURAL SUPPORT SYSTEMS V. ORGANIZATIONAL STRUCTURE

The problems of primary groups or natural support systems have become increasingly important both in social science research and in social policy. In part, the community mental health program was founded on the assumption that natural support systems or some analogue of them could more effectively take over many of the life support activities of the large state mental hospitals and, in addition, provide a better mental health milieu for the patient. For instance, the assumption was that the mentally ill could be taken care of by their families, neighbors, a foster family, or even live by themselves with some outpatient help from a community mental health center, rather than live in a state institution. Such living arrangements could more easily meet the idiosyncratic everyday living needs of the elderly as well as promote better state mental health. Though the principles of this rationale were often not spelled out, later work on the roles of primary groups did suggest some important principles. Most activities such as eating, leisure, protection, physical medicine, mental health, and the like, have some aspects which require either technical knowledge or large-scale resources to implement. At the same time, they have certain aspects which require primary groups or the natural support system. People who were put in large state mental institutions lost out in the latter area. By putting individuals back in the community and providing them with close liaison with the community mental health center, the implicit hope was to permit patients to have the resources of both the formal organization and the natural support systems.

To illustrate, the large-scale institution can ensure that everyone will eat by providing three meals a day. However, it can do this only by providing very standardized meals—everyone must eat much the same thing at fixed times and places. By contrast, the natural support system can often tailor the menu, the time, and the place to the desires of its members—though it cannot necessarily give as strong a guarantee that three meals a day will be provided. In the same way, it can be argued that the formal organization can guarantee standardized leisure activities, standardized medical care, standardized protection against theft, standardized mental health services, but it has a much harder time dealing with the idiosyncratic needs of patients, especially those requiring little physical resource. Thus the natural support system can give better home nursing care, tailored to the unique needs of the member. It can provide every day tension management to deal with the unique and everyday problems of its members. It can select the form of entertainment most likely to please its members (movies, television, music, or rides in the country). The reason for the superiority of the natural support sytsems is twofold. For the large formal institution to function effectively it must have economies on a large scale. To effect such economies it must routinize activities. Thus, the only way two or three people can feed 100 is by making a single, standardized meal, and by insisting that everyone eat at one time and in one place. The only way one nurse's aide can take the temperature of ten people in five to ten minutes is by insisting that they all wake up at the same time. The only way the housekeeping staff can have a few people change the sheets and clean the rooms is to insist that this be done at clearly specified days and times.

In other words, given a small staff and a large number of clients, it is to the staff's interest to routinize the patients' life as much as possible if they are to do their job with efficiency. It is, however, this very routinization of life that works against the effort to provide distinctive care for the patient, e.g., food to match his taste, nursing care adapted to his idiosyncratic needs, intimate companions with whom to talk about everyday trials and joys, and so forth. The natural support systems, by virtue of their size, can provide these idiosyncratic needs. It is not only a question of size but, in addition, one of the true primary group or natural sytem having noninstrumental ties to each other. People do things because their relationship is an end in itself. Parents do things for their children, not to gain some advantage, but because they are children. By contrast, for the large institution to run effectively, it must stress more instrumental relations. That is, if the cook or the doctor are incompetent they must be removed. If they have noninstrumental ties such as those of the family, doctors and staff would be chosen not on their ability but rather on the basis of the likes and dislikes for each other. The large-scale system assumes that all clients will be treated equally by the staff. With a small staff and many patients it is impossible for the staff to develop the close ties that they have with their family members. If the staff develops ties with some, but not with others, then problems of unequal treatment would emerge, with only the favored clients obtaining good service. Furthermore, if staff involvement gets too close to the clients, and there is turnover in clients or staff, there may be another difficulty: The staff and the clients would be faced with the prospect of forming close ties with people who would be continually leaving. In the case of the elderly, where leaving might mean death, then the question must be asked, how can the staff continually bear losing dear ones to death, or how can the older people bear continually losing close friends or family members (staff) who had only a limited time commitment to their job.

The large organization also gains its effectiveness through the use of specialized and highly technical knowledge. Where people are closely tied emotionally, they might not use this technical knowledge objectively. For instance, doctors are urged not to treat close relatives (or themselves) for major medical problems, just as lawyers are urged to hire an attorney if they need major legal aid.

In other words, to do its job properly and to ensure equal treatment of its clients, the large, formal organization must operate on a far more instrumental basis than the small, primary group or the natural support system. It is, however, this very noninstrumental relation of the small support group which permits it to handle the idiosyncratic aspects of goal achievement. These aspects and goals are often very hard to observe. If people take on these idiosyncratic tasks for expediency, that is, if they are paid to handle them, and the tasks are hard to observe, then there is a good chance that the tasks will not be performed effectively. Where the job is not easily observable and there is no way to evaluate the outcome, then expediency would dictate that people do as little as possible. For instance, a nurses aide is hired to watch a patient when no one will be home or during the night when everyone is asleep. When the tasks involve things like bringing cold water to the patient, or moving the patient so that bed sores will not develop, or saying reassuring things so that the patient will not worry, or encouraging a patient to eat, or changing his dressings, then the nurse's aide might not do these things completely since it is often difficult or impossible to judge how well such tasks are being handled without continuous observation. The nurses aide can always be "nice" while being observed and then change when no one is present. But, where there is a deep, personal involvement (people with a noninstrumental orientation) then the person handling these tasks will do them regardless of economic reward and lack of organization. In other words, natural support systems, because of their non-economic motive, often better perform these idiosyncratic jobs.

It is not only that small size permits one to tailor tasks, and that noninstrumental ties permit one to work in situations where it is hard to motivate others, but these natural support systems often involve long-term relations in which people get to know each other's idiosyncrasies very well. The natural support member may know what to say to comfort a sick patient, while the nurses aide might not. The natural support system member might know what the individual likes to read, might know the idiosyncratic factor that effects moods (e.g., grumpy in morning), or the peculiar ways of expressing pain.

In other words, the very structure of the natural support systems or primary groups (their small size, their noninstrumental relations, their stress on positive affect, and their long-term commitments) permit them to handle idiosyncratic tasks not requiring high states of knowledge—and to do so more effectively than the staff of large institutions. Furthermore, the economies of large scale that make the large institutions so useful, often mean that the staff cannot engage to the same extent in such relationships without threatening these economies.

There is a second point which suggests why it is that in principle one should move people out of large institutional settings. The delineation of group properties highlights the contradictions in the demands of large, formal institutions and natural support systems. To effect large scale economies and to have technical experts available, an organization must stress size, routinization of tasks, impersonal objective relations, shorter time commitments, and more segmental ties. All things being equal, if one wants to maximize both the standardized and nonstandardized parts of goal achievement, then it is generally wise to separate the structures for handling technical tasks and economies of large scale from those handling idiosyncratic and nontechnical tasks. In a large, formal institution where clients live 24 hours a day, it is most difficult to have both of these groups operating simultaneously. We repeat. It is most difficult, not impossible. There are indeed ways to do so even in a 24-hour, live-in situation, but there is a substantial cost. All things being equal, it generally costs less to separate the formal and the natural support system. It is these considerations that provide the treatment philosophy of the community mental health centers. This is not to deny that many others saw such centers as an opportunity to save money by closing down expensive state mental hospitals and had no idea one way or the other of the consequence to mental health patients. This latter factor may have accounted for the speed with which this movement was implemented by legislation.

The philosophy of natural support systems and formal organizations has many obvious problems. First, since both are essential to the achievement of most goals, it raises the question of how to coordinate the two groups once they are separated. The concept of the community mental health centers implied the principle that decentralized services close to the community would make for good coordination. But it turned out that coordination was far more complicated. The exact procedures for effecting coordination between the centers and their communities is a major topic of research which we hope to highlight later.

But a second and equally important problem is to discover the properties of the natural support system and to determine which one would be good for which type of idiosyncratic task. Thus, one can choose between something like a conjugal unit (husband and wife), a kinship unit (husband and wife and relative), neighbors, friends, cooperative living arrangements, halfway houses, various forms of families with partial services provided at home (such as homekeeping services and visiting nurses). Thus, one of the major research problems arising from such an approach is an effort to determine what are the best natural support systems and which system is appropriate for which type of task.

This problem becomes especially obvious when dealing with the aged population: One characteristic of the aged population is the impairment of physical abilities. It means that many tasks which were handled by the natural support system can no longer be so handled. For instance, because of physical infirmities older persons might not be able to dress themselves,

to cook, to shop or buy their own clothes, to take transportation to the doctor or movies or church. If there is a virtue in
maintaining some natural support system, as the above principles suggest, the question arises, can services be brought in to
maintain those with such infirmities in the community? If so,
which group should undertake the services of feeding, trans-
porting, housekeeping, and so forth? Should it be kin, friends,
neighbors, or some stranger from an indigenous culture?

In considering the natural support systems as superior to
state mental health facilities, there were two major issues
involved. First, the natural support systems can deliver many
of the same services (cooking, leisure activities, housing) as
the state hospital. It can do so more effectively and at less cost
to society. Equally important was an argument that such living
conditions would have a curative effect on the mental health
of the patient. For many psychiatrists, putting the patient into
a normal role is a major part of his cure. It is important to
differentiate the effective delivery of services (e.g., patients
eating the food they like) and the curative role of living in the
community from costs. In the short run, these outcomes might
not be correlated with costs. Thus, studies may show that it is
more expensive to maintain community mental health services
and their support systems than state mental health hospitals
even though it is also true that the former are better for many
patients. A study that compares the costs of state mental
hospitals and community mental health centers and the rate of
mental health "cures" would be most interesting.

To understand the full fiscal implications of such a study,
however, it is necessary to consider one other aspect of deinstitutionalization: the need to establish a series of coordinate
services to complement the mental health centers. Thus, to
put the client in a natural support system leaves open the
question of how does one ensure that the client has adequate
medical services, leisure time or recreational facilities, protection, nutrition, legal protection, housing, and shopping
facilities. In a state mental hospital all of these facilities and

their services were the responsibility of one organization, the hospital. But, in the outer community, each of these services may have its own institutional source. How does the community mental health movement ensure that such services will be provided? So important has this question become, that many former advocates of deinstitutionalization have questioned its consequences for the aged. They find older people often located in nursing homes that have few of the institutional services provided by state mental health hospitals, and they ask if the movement for deinstitutionalization has, in fact, led to reinstitutionalization on a far less adequate level. Whatever the virtues of the natural system, they should not be purchased at the cost of important institutional services as medical care and housing.

This concern of many investigators has often been reflected in the organizational dilemmas confronting the staff of community mental health centers. These dilemmas concern the question of what should and should not be included in the community mental health centers. Should they include within their buildings not only mental health but physical health, housing services, various social work services, legal services, and police services? Even where it is not a question of having these services under one roof, there might be great concern as to how the community mental health center should coordinate with these various services. In this regard, the question arises as how best to ensure that the aged are included as a group. This raises questions of organizational structure in which the solutions vary from the extreme of having special centers for the aged, to having departments within a center, to having a person within the center, to having a general mandate with no specific person assigned to the aging. How to best ensure center concentration on aging is again a key research question.

There is yet another very important implication: As the community mental health movement has developed, and as studies of aging have developed, it is clear that, depending on the nature of the client, not only are different forms of natural

support systems necessary but also different degrees of institutionalization. The older person who needs 24-hour care over
long periods may be too much for any natural support system.
Perhaps the older, senile patient who has lost control of bodily
functions may need institutionalization. But, there are degrees
of formalization. Thus some people who are so physically
infirm that they cannot perform any of the everyday tasks of
living might have some semi-institutional services rendered in
their own residence. Only tasks of daily living could be taken
care of by the institution on the analogy of some hotel services.
Where people are not able to do the household cleaning but
are still able to cook, then a slightly different version might be
acceptable. In short, it is clear, especially with older people,
that different infirmities require different forms of institutionalization; the natural support systems do not have the large-
scale resources to manage some of these activities.

There are two major research problems connected with this
issue. First, there is need systematically to study types of
infirmities and care systems to find out which range of the
population might ideally be handled by community mental
health centers and which by more institutionalized forms of
care. Second, there is a need to study how natural support
systems relate to more institutional settings. For instance,
there is increasing evidence that older people in homes for the
aged or retirement homes do much better if they have kin who
visit. The dilemma of institutions not being able to handle the
more idiosyncratic aspects of living can be solved by moving
people out of the institution. Where people cannot be moved,
then it must be solved by bringing the natural support systems
to the institutions.

There is a further pair of problems: how the community
ensures that the center is following its policy directives, and
how the community ensures that the center staff are not abus-
ing their positions. It should be understood that all institutions
are guided by policy considerations that do not necessarily
involve technical matters but reflect community values. They
often have boards composed of lay people whose purpose is to

reflect significant community values. For instance, school systems may have boards of education composed of lay people, business corporations may have boards of directors representing stock holders, and social work agencies may have boards of directors representing the community. Most city agencies have as heads politically appointed individuals who are supposed to reflect the policy of elected officials and their community mandates; the agencies of the federal government are all headed by political appointees.

In schools, the decisions about more courses in music, sports, science or history, about prayer in the classroom, about integration or segregation, are decisions which depend to a considerable extent on the values of the community and not on technical expertise. The field of community mental health may have many value decisions which should be rightfully made by the community but which the experts may or may not acknowledge as value problems. For instance, the community, through its legislators, has now mandated that community mental health should include treatment of the aged as one of its specific services. In many centers there may be a question as to whether community mental health programs should concentrate on prevention or immediate treatment. If programs differ in the short run, should they give greater priority to a few who are seriously ill or to many with minor illnesses? Should they concentrate on treatment which provides low costs, thus permitting society to use its money for other goals? Or should it concentrate on treatments with high costs even though this may require society to pull money from other fields? If natural support systems are more costly but more effective, should they be supported? If a choice has to be made between services to the elderly or to children, who should make this choice? To these policy questions must also be added the question of abuse by staff. If the community has decided policy in one direction and the staff does not carry it out, who is to monitor staff refusal and ensure that something is done about it? If the staff takes advantage of its position to mistreat patients, who will ensure that the patients' charges are heard?

These questions raise a corresponding set of research issues. To what extent, if any, are lay people represented in policy positions in the mental health center? If they are, to what extent do they represent the clientele? For instance, if the aged are the clientele, to what extent are the aged on such boards or are those who have a vested interest in the aged, that is, the relatives of the aged? To what extent do key client groups have autonomous organizations which ensure continued client pressure even when they are not on the board? To what extent do client groups have available, either through their own organizations or others in the community, resources to bring in outside technical expertise if they feel that the staff is not performing its tasks correctly? For instance, are there organizations of the aged or their kin with sufficient resources to hire a lawyer and bring suit if they feel mental health centers are not meeting their obligation under the law to service the aged? Are there organizations that can hire doctors to show that the medical staff of the center is systematically misdiagnosing problems of the aged or are indifferent to their treatment?

RESEARCH ON DECENTRALIZATION

Community mental health centers are decentralized so that clients may have easy access. However, the question arises concerning how far they can be decentralized. New York City may have approximately ten centers for its 8 million people. Utilization studies at analogous, decentralized services suggest that people in the immediate vicinity may use them as originally envisioned. For those living at a considerable distance, however, only those who are wealthy, physically vigorous, and highly motivated are likely to use them. Because many elderly suffer a physical decline, services must be close by, or chauffering must be available, or some aggressive outreach program must include them. In addition, older people in American society tend to be poor. These two attributes suggest that older people specifically will be one of the groups heavily affected by the inability to establish mental health centers on an extensively decentralized basis, e.g., a block unit. We need studies to show where center users live, and what are their economic, physical, and mental conditions. We need to know to what extent decentralization of these centers is important, and to see if indeed older people are one of several significant groups who are excluded by lack of proximity.

The same problem can be approached experimentally. We need centers of varying degrees of decentralization with some deliberately performing as storefront services that would locate them near their potential clientele. Others would be more centralized in a district, while still others would retain even greater centralization. These studies should not only determine what populations are reached by each degree of decentralization, but, in addition, what services each can offer and at what cost in manpower and facilities. The cost of each solution, if they were expanded as a national policy, should be determined. Thus, one possible cost would be the inability to use medical tools requiring large-scale economies. In other words, surgical facilities, X-ray machines, and labs, require large populations and large expenditures of money for efficient use. Also, decentralization usually means smaller staffs that generally preclude the same degree of specialization of large central institutions.

Perhaps a more sophisticated experiment would be one establishing a system of services with some, very small, satellite storefront centers to handle initial diagnosis and emergency treatment. Treatment requiring only limited resources with a large centralized community center could handle problems of longer duration. An experimental study providing such a setup and comparing it with one that has only the centralized (or the decentralized), or what is typical of current centers, would be illuminating. To the extent that these variations already exist, what is needed is a systematic comparison of the kinds of people reached (e.g., the nature of the problem and the resource).

Decentralization was one aspect of a larger theme: The center must reach populations often overlooked because they lacked resources. As a consequence, a concern of the mental health centers was the extent to which they used links to the community that involved actively reaching out (e.g., home visits) and the extent to which the services they provided should involve experts or more indigenous people with moderate training or people with less training. Thus, the community mental health centers can reach their clientele by insisting that people come to the center for help; they can reach into the home of the client by sending visiting nurses or providing homemaking services. They can also establish voluntary associations to chauffeur clients to the center, or they can hire indigenous people to carry the center's message to the clients. They can make use of the mass media, or they can rely on formal organizations such as the police, hospitals, and social work agencies to refer clients to them.

These are all links to the community. Rather than speak about the degree of decentralization of the community mental health center, it is possible to suggest that centers can vary their distance from the clients by types of links to the community. Decentralization is only one procedure. Such links can generally be evaluated by four crucial properties. First, to what extent do they leave the initiative to the center staff, and to what extent do they leave the initiative in the hands of the client? Thus, if the community mental health staff sought to reach frail elderly (those who, because of mental or physical problems, are afraid to leave their house) by sending mental health specialists into their homes, then the center staff has the initiative. If the staff decides to reach such clients by use of mass media, however, then the initiative lies in the hands of the client whether the message will be heard. The more decentralized community mental health centers are, the higher the staff initiative. Voluntary associations generally mean low staff initiative. But where the centers have contacts with police, hospitals, and social work agencies who are very likely to be in contact with people with mental health problems, and those professionals in turn have a commitment to turn such clients over to the center staff, then the staff will have initiative through these other agencies. But if the community mental health center has no such commitment, then such secondary recruitment results in low staff initiative. In general, the more passive the client (physically infirm, poor, mentally ill), then the more the staff must use links which have high initiative. The wealthier, more physically robust, and mentally healthy the client, the more the staff can use links with low initiative.

A second issue is the degree of technical expertise necessary to deliver services. Where mental health problems arise because the individual finds he can no longer manage everyday living, or where the doctor feels that the mental health of patients will be materially improved if they are put into a milieu where they must engage in normal everyday activities, then it is quite possible that the linkage will not require high states of technical expertise. For instance, where an elderly person is suffering major problems because he or she can no longer cook a meal because their physical infirmities prevent them from using public transportation and shopping, then the treatment of choice may be using volunteers either to drive the elderly person to a store or to do the shopping for them. This may require a link which involves an indigenous nonexpert with modest, specialized training. The idea is to get someone who is sufficiently close to the elderly person in culture to understand his or her food preferences and who can communicate easily with him or her. On the other hand, the link to the elderly person may require some highly skilled, technically trained person. For instance, if, through a prolonged period of isolation elderly people have developed a fear of strangers as well as the fear of leaving their homes, then it may be necessary for a highly skilled clinician to communicate with them and to change their orientation. Sometimes the link may require simultaneous technical training and indigenous knowledge.

It should be understood that the problems of staff initiative may exist independently of the question of whether the agency is to provide technical expertise or nontechnical resources. One can have linkage mechanisms that have outreach and technical (visiting nurse) or nontechnical resources (homemaker) as well as linkages that are passive and have technical (center-based therapy by professional therapist) or nontechnical resources (center-based, client-leisure "therapy" groups).

Yet another dimension of linkage is the extent that it enables one to deal with many or few people. Sometimes the staff would like to deal only with a few people such as those cases where one-to-one intensive psychotherapy is necessary. Other times staff may want wider links such as trying to recruit volunteers to chauffeur or visit the aged. Linkages vary in the number of people they reach; the mass media reach many, while the intensive home visit, such as in aggressive casework, reaches few. Using the wrong linkage can result in too many, too few, or the wrong type of clients. Thus, when one agency sought to reach only the frail aged, they advertised through the mass media and received too many people of the wrong kind. The robust aged came. On the other hand, if one is developing a program of volunteers to drive the aged to various agencies for services or to provide them with companionship, one might want a wide linkage. Using linkages such as home visits for recruiting people would waste staff time. The mass media would be far more effective.

Finally, such linkages can be evaluated by the extent to which they force staff and clients into close, primary group relations. As noted above, where staff and client become too closely involved, the staff may lose its objectivity or the client may become too instrumentally oriented. Thus, in dealing with the aged the staff may become so involved with a particular client that they ignore others and avoid professional decisions which may be necessary but which may involve moving the client from their jurisdiction. On the other hand, professionals dealing with kin of relatives may so overwhelm them that the kin pay attention only to technical aspects of their care and lose sight of the fact that the person they are dealing with is an elderly parent who requires some love and affection and whose idiosyncratic needs must be met as well. The community mental health centers with their stress on decentralization and outreach programs may run such risks more than traditional institutional programs. In general, too much contact and loss of objectivity is not yet a major problem. The literature stresses the problem of too much distance. Problems of too much closeness, however, have arisen in other fields that use highly decentralized services, volunteers, and indigenous staff. In such situations staff are often under enormous pressure to behave in noninstrumental (nepotistic) ways with clients. Where health centers are successful in developing extreme decentralization for the aged and the extensive use of volunteers and indigenous staff, the problems of too much closeness and role conflict will become significant.

Given the above considerations, any linkage used by the community mental health centers can be evaluated by four properties, and, as a consequence, something can be said about what kinds of services will be delivered to what kinds of clientele. All too often agencies become committed to a particular type of linkage and, as a consequence, do not recognize that they may be missing certain clients or particular forms of mental illness.

Thus, an agency which relies only on its position as a community mental health center and occasional mass medium will have very low staff initiative. As a consequence, they are very likely to systematically overlook all elderly people who are too infirm to travel on their own, who are mentally too ill to come in on their own, who have a negative orientation toward mental health or are economically too poor to come in on their own, or who lack strong natural support systems to bring them in.

A community mental health center that relies heavily on a highly trained technical staff might not deal with mental health problems that can be easily solved by providing services of nonexpert indigenous people to compensate for loss of function of the aged, for example, visiting to break isolation, providing peers for interaction as a part of therapy, aiding in household tasks to relieve the anxiety of everyday living, and so forth.

Given such principles, community mental health centers should be examined to see what linkages they in fact use and what populations they are reaching. It would be important to see if it is indeed true that different linkages recruit different clients with different problems.

An important adjunct to this, especially if community mental health centers do not have much variation in the use of linkages, would be an experimental study in which community mental health centers would deliberately vary the forms of linkages they used to see if this would produce different kinds of clientele. Designing such an experimental project would entail a far greater specification of clients and treatment than can be undertaken here. In the field of aging, however, the generic problem suggests certain obvious cases, and one such experiment will be outlined. One agency might engage in intensive outreach programs with much staff initiative and high use of indigenous and expert staff, while another might concentrate on a more passive program with a high concentration on staff expertise, while still another might concentrate more on working with other organizations to coordinate their services. The first variation would concentrate on the fact that physical infirmities prevent many aged from coming into the program. It is an extreme statement of the need to close distance. The second variation is a recognition that many of the elderly in need of help are sufficiently robust or have sufficiently strong support systems so they can be brought to the center. This saves precious staff time and permits the use of more specialized people and facilities; for example, overnight emergency facilities. The third approach suggests that mental health resources are too limited, and to maximize their use one should take advantage of other agencies. For instance, clergymen, teachers, police, regular medical doctors, and mailmen are all in occupations that have regular contacts with people. If they can be trained to diagnose symptoms and steer people to mental health facilities, or if they can be trained in preventive approaches, it could expand the resources of mental health. These three designs involve different linkages with different properties and presumably should attract different clients with different problems and resources. It is important to demonstrate this systematically if one is to choose among the alternatives.

More generally, centers could introduce experimental variation in any of the dimensions of linkage-outreach, expertise-indigenous, scope, and degree of role conflict.

TYPES OF SYSTEMS AND ALTERNATIVES

Yet another important area of research is a comparative study of the types of natural support systems to see which are more appropriate for what circumstances. One of the major factors affecting aging is physical disability and death that disrupts the family—husband and wife. As a consequence, if the elderly are to remain in the community they require some form of support. Instances of this kind of support are programs of home nursing care, homemaker services, and meals on wheels that some agencies have developed. In addition, they have developed programs that encourage relatives, neighbors, and friends to help the aged.

Such services are an agency's effort to strengthen or duplicate the activities of the natural support system. This in turn leads to a series of research questions worth stating explicitly. The first is a study to understand the limits and resources of various natural support systems. What in principle can the kinship unit do? What can the neighborhood unit do? What can the peer group do? To what extent can their functions be carried on by the other, and to what extent can agencies provide functional alternatives? The initial research data provide some suggestions. Kin have long-term commitments to the subject. Neighbors have immediate access and deal with problems requiring geographical proximity but not necessarily long-term commitments. Peers who are friends have the unique understanding of the problems of aging that ensures a communality of interest as well as a unique ability to communicate about leisure activities and problems. Thus, the kinship system can take care of an aged relative for illnesses that require some home nursing care. Neighbors can ward off muggers, warn the police if the house or apartment is being burglarized, exchange information on inexpensive places to shop, and so forth. Peers can share the common problems of dealing with social security. They can likewise share common views on leisure-time activities that depend on common physical limits and generational norms. These would include types of dances, movies, and reading material they enjoy in common. Peers also provide each other with companionship during that part of the day when the rest of the population is involved in the occupational world. Peers of the aged, however, may be too frail and too economically depressed to undertake home nursing care or to aid friends to go to the doctor's office or to aid in shopping.

For each of these groups one might have a paid substitute. Thus the agency can pay individuals to provide meals for aged persons, to drive them to the hospital, or to be a companion. Finally, in each of these cases the question might arise as to whether the agency can find a volunteer to handle these problems who is not necessarily a neighbor, kin, or peer.

The research question here can be approached through a survey of ongoing families and agencies or through an experimental-field demonstration approach. The field study might be that of older people under different states of disability to determine which types of informal support systems they use for which type of problems and what, if any, are the outcomes. Alternatively, one might approach various mental health centers and cooperative agencies to stress these experimental approaches to cover a multiplicity of problems. One approach would concentrate on developing and building kinship ties for the older person, the second would organize neighbors to aid the older person, while the third would organize peers. A series of standardized outcomes would be measured before and after to see which of these areas the various natural support systems are able to handle best. The standardized outcomes will be (1) a handling problem requiring long term commitment, such as home nursing help for a week or more; (2) problems involving immediate time emergencies requiring geographical proximity, for example, providing aid if an elderly person is wandering in the street seriously disoriented; (3) and problems of elderly people who have become depressed through extreme isolation, inability to find others with mutual interests and common physical and economic limits. These illustrate only the class of problems under each rubric.

When considering the possibility of paid versus nonpaid natural support systems, it is necessary to take into account that many of the services provided by the natural support system involve highly idiosyncratic, unpredictable tasks. To perform them with success, one needs detailed knowledge of the individual involved which often means a long association and a form of commitment which is noninstrumental. Because the successful carrying out of these tasks is often not observable it cannot easily be evaluated by an outside source. As a consequence, those who work only for expediency can often perform slackly without fear of discovery. For instance, a company which provides a meal on wheels may not know the special foods that the clients need, the specific time of day they would like to eat, the extent to which they like to eat with others or alone, whether they like to eat watching a favorite television program, and the extent to which they must be encouraged or motivated to eat.

It is true that members of the natural support system may generally be more knowledgeable and more motivated. They might not, however, have the resources to help an aged parent if the nature of the tasks requires more time and energy than is ordinarily expended in natural support systems. On the other hand, if they are paid so that they can be released from other tasks, then it raises another problem. How can one retain the noninstrumental relationship of the natural support system if one is getting paid?

Here is a suggested experimental study. A selected agency will systematically compare people who require aid beyond that typically available in a natural support system. The agency will try one program where they pay natural support systems to help the aged member (for example, money paid to neighbors, relatives, and peers) and compare this with a program that pays individuals who are indigenous but not members of the support system. This in turn is compared with situations where natural support systems are used without aid. This experimental design could be elaborated by separating the different types of natural support systems.

Natural support systems have yet another problem. If we examine neighborhoods we find many different kinds. Some neighborhoods ("mobility neighborhoods") are organized even though they have members moving in and out. These would contrast with traditional neighborhoods where people remain their entire life. In turn, they can be contrasted with mass neighborhoods where people may move but do not explicitly exchange with each other. These can be contrasted with volatile neighborhoods where sub groups are in basic conflict. There is some basis for arguing that the mobile neighborhoods are the only ones able to meet the demands of a modern industrial society. People can move for occupational reasons and to take advantage of better technology for building houses and to increase prosperity. Society is free for maximum choice in planning, and people are free to move in response to changes in their family life cycle.

Some of these concerns are especially important for the aged. Some aged are concentrated in homogeneous peer group communities that permit them to take advantage of neighborhood services specifically designed for the aged. Examples would be a local clinic specializing in gerontology, recreational activities for the aged, neighbors on common time schedules who can look after each other, and traffic regulations to accommodate the infirmities of old age. Such peer group neighborhoods are characterized by high mobility; neighbors are removed by death or illnesses resulting in institutionalization.

Some aged live in mixed aged groups. The changes mentioned above often leave the aged isolated among groups with different cultures. Thus poor, white elderly may end up living among blacks or Spanish-Americans.

Might people living in mobility neighborhoods, either mixed or homogeneous, have advantages over people living in traditional or mass neighborhoods? If this is true then it becomes very important to understand how practitioners can aid people in organizing their neighborhoods from one type to another. For instance, one of the key features of the mobility neighborhoods is their quick modes of integrating people into the group. How does one train people in the use of these mechanisms? A series of experimental studies on how neighborhoods of different types can be altered to make them more effective in dealing with problems of mobility and the larger society would be in order.

Along parallel lines there are alternative views on what constitutes an ideal kinship system. If a kinship system is to function in a modern society it must not lead to major social forms of nepotism in the labor force and must permit people to move freely geographically and occupationally without having as a matter of course to take kin along with them. This raises the question of how kin systems can survive where they are not geographically or occupationally close. The traditional kinship system rejected differential mobility. Therefore, ties to the traditional kinship groups may often lead individuals to suffer economically (and experience unnecessary guilt as well) when put between the demands of the occupational world and that of the kinship system. Traditional kinship systems often forced individuals to choose between complete aid or no aid. Thus it was viewed as responsible for all aspects of a person's life, job, housing, education, medical care, and so forth. In contemporary society, however, large scale organizations undertake these activities too, that is, social security systems for payment of income to elderly people, hospitals and Medicaid for medical problems, police for protection, and so on. It has been argued that, for a modern kinship system to be effectively used it must learn to exchange only in the non-technical areas and with small resources, leaving the large resources to the formal organizations.

The modern kinship system must learn both the lesson of partial exchange vis-à-vis the large organization and the concept of partial aid vis-à-vis its own conjugal subunits. Thus the idea is a series of semiautonomous, conjugal subunits rather than the traditional kinship system that ideally was a single unit with one head having power over the subunits in all areas of life. The problem of maintaining a confederation of conjugal subunits is very different from that of maintaining a group with a single authority head. The key to the former is the need to exchange without the donor dominating the recipient. Thus the modern kinship unit must stress exchanges that involve reciprocity; exchanges made on institutional occasions when the donor cannot expect influence to go with the gift; multiple units for exchange, so the recipient has more than one kinship unit to go to if the donor demands too much; and some way to adjudicate disputes if one does not have a single authority with major power.

One of the major interesting studies is to see which, if any, type of kinship units—the modified extended family or the traditional one—will best provide aid in the modern society. For the mental health therapist who finds kinship ties to be one of the major sources of anxiety, it provides a positive model or ideal type to aim for. The alternative is to be faced either with the isolated nuclear unit or the traditional ones. Should kin feel guilty or not guilty about putting an elderly person in a home for the aged? Should a kin system try to maintain the elderly in the community even if they have to sacrifice their own conjugal units? Are there services that the kinship unit can provide even when elderly are put into nursing homes? Though there are interesting beginnings in research which suggest that the elderly get better care where kin visit nursing home facilities, and that there are many things that kin can provide that staff cannot, this research is just beginning and must be elaborated if practitioners are to use them for therapy or training guides.

In this regard we can see experimental situations where mental health centers might seek specifically to train kinship units to communicate across geographical and occupational distance, to limit their exchanges to the nontechnical areas and small economies, and to exchange with each other under norms of reciprocity and nondominance.

In American society, friendship groups generally are considered to be among peers. What characterizes such groups among the aged is that the peers are frail and generally have few economic resources. As a consequence, peer friends among the aged have short life spans. This means that the aged must either assume that they will not have any friends or that they must continually form new friends as old ones die or become seriously ill. This raises a research question concerning quick socialization which can ensure friendship despite short term commitments. It is a problem that confronts neighborhoods which are highly mobile as well. The two phenomena may differ, however, in that the friendship groups may not have the same geographical proximity.

The issue of short term commitments may also radically alter the meaning of friendship. One may not be able to ask the same things of older friends as contrasted with younger ones. One of the major virtues of such peer friendship groups is that they share many common interests, so that there is a strong incentive to keep together. Who else can understand the frustrations of not being able to shop or use public transportation? Who else has a daily routine which permits the degree of leisure and social activities? Who else can understand the common institutions one must deal with, such as Social Security, as well as the common reactions from younger people to an elder's slower reflexes? Who else can understand the benefits of specialized services to the aged?

On the other hand, the extreme frailty of the friendship ties of age peers means that activities requiring physical strength or economic resources, or long term commitments might not be easily undertaken by elderly groups.

A key research question is to compare the aged with friends of the same or older generation with those having younger friends to see what each can and cannot do. This is an area that has received more research than many of the others previously mentioned, but often the researchers were not as precisely focused on problems of friendship and what it is that each group can do. But, in addition, the question arises about the extent to which peer groups of the same age can be developed by agency support to deal with problems of long term commitments, and to what extent can cross-age friendships be buttressed to deal with the specialized problems of each age group as well.

In this regard a consideration of the differing use of these various forms of natural support systems with the changing state of health of the older person is also an important problem. When the aged are robust, then the same-aged friendship groups and neighborhoods can have enormous benefits. When the aged become more frail, then it may become necessary to move to kinship systems and friendship groups which involve cross-generational ties. Thus studies which compare and contrast the nature of natural support systems at different stages of health would be of great import. In this regard, experimental studies in which agencies concentrated on developing cross-aged natural support systems for those who are ill and the same-aged natural support systems for those who are robust would be of some interest. These experimental groups would be contrasted with the aged who have only the same-aged peers when they are ill or well and those having only cross-generational ties when they are ill and well.

There are two areas of the natural support system which will not be developed herein but should be researched. First, one should consider in much greater detail nonpaid and nonrelated volunteers. There is some confusion in the field concerning the extent to which they can be substituted for natural support systems such as the family, neighbors, or friends. It is our initial hypothesis that the kinds of tasks which the natural support systems best handle include those that require deep personal involvement and long term commitments, because they often involve onerous duties and much energy. One can speculate that there are few volunteers that have this kind of motivation and time to commit to "strangers." As a consequence, volunteer programs which seek to replace regular activities of natural support systems with nonpaid, volunteer "strangers" will have to be very small, for they must rely on heroic people. By contrast, there are many jobs that the natural support systems handles which are short term and require no large time commitment nor are they onerous, such as the job of driving people to the doctor's office or helping people write letters or dial a phone. For these kinds of activities volunteers of the "stranger" type can be developed into a very large program.

Another line of research which should be encouraged but which has not been developed here involves the husband and wife dyadic relationship. There are several ideal role models in modern industrial society. One is the traditional sexually linked division of labor. The other is the notion of equality and role substitutability. The latter assumes that modern technology results in many things being taken out and put into the family during its existence. As a consequence, husband and wife cannot rely on a standardized division of labor but must continually be prepared to shift roles. Such shifts may result in both doing the same thing or a traditional division of labor or a reverse division of labor or some entirely new division of labor. This becomes especially relevant to the problems of the aged where the husband's retirement and the illness of one or the other spouse may require the man to keep house or the wife to assume the outside, instrumental roles. It would be of enormous interest to see if marriages using a role substitutability are better able to manage the stresses and strains of retirement than those who have a traditional role model. In addition, such role substitutability models have their own stresses and strains which tend to focus on how rapidly people can learn new roles as well as how people manage with inconsistent roles. A series of studies along these lines would be of great importance for those seeking to deal with natural support systems, mental health, and the problems of aging. This suggests a study in which, prior to retirement, some families are given intensive training in role substitutability. They could then be compared with families who proceeded with their natural role division to see which group was better able to handle the stress of retirement.

ORGANIZATIONAL STRUCTURES: CENTRALIZATION OF AUTHORITY

The community mental health services have traditionally provided outpatient care, some partial hospitalization, emergency treatment, inpatient care and consultation, and education. In addition, within these categories they may have varying treatments, calling for some kind of individual or group therapy. Within this context, new legislation has included the demand that centers must now include treatment of the aged. The question arises in organizations which have multiple tasks or alternative modes for achieving the same task of how to ensure that each will be equally emphasized. Alternatively, if there is some hierarchy of tasks, how does one ensure that the hierarchy stated is the one which will be implemented? There are many different ways of studying this problem and here we will concentrate on the organizational factors which affect the degree to which a given task or alternative will be stressed.

One of the chief factors to be considered in organizational theory is the degree to which the structure of the organization is set up with a single centralized authority. For instance, a mental health center can be set up with a strong central administrator who participates to a major extent in personal and program decisions in all areas. Such organizational structures are often characterized by a lack of strong departments or departments which are set up for administrative purposes on the basis of rules but where effective decision-making or policy is kept firmly in the hands of the chief administrator. By contrast, organizations can be set up with strong, autonomous units where the administrator plays more the role of coordinator and adjudicator but where the basic personnel and program decisions are made within the departments. In the extreme case, a given service may be even physically detached from the rest. To make this point clear, the services for the aged could be separated from the rest of the community mental health centers in a separate satellite structure with a general budget which, in turn, can be allocated as suits personnel and program needs. This would be an extremely decentralized authority. A next stage might be a department within the center which is set up with special personnel for dealing with the aged, has a standardized budget commitment, and has considerable freedom to develop its own program and personnel policies; the rest of the center staff would have only veto power. A lesser form of decentralization might be the hiring of specific individuals (in no separate department) for handling problems of the aged. All major program decisions would have to be cleared through some central executive. Perhaps the extreme form of centralization would be one in which there is no specified person or department set up for the aged but only a generalized mandate that all people handle problems of aging, and it is the chief executive of the center who will determine personnel problems and program policy. Obviously we have not dealt with all possibilities (for instance, the use of committees) nor have we separated the problems of authority and degree of specialization.

Another key organizational factor where one has many tasks or alternatives is the degree to which they are competitive or facilitatively related to each other. For instance, given the limits of funds, the more a given community mental health program concentrates on crisis intervention, the less funds it might have for regular outpatient treatment. The more a center concentrates on consultation and education, the less funds it may have for crisis intervention. These illustrate the tasks that are competitively interdependent—the more one is stressed, the less the other is stressed. In other cases, services and alternatives might be facilitatively related, that is, the more successful one is, the more successful the other. For instance, staff can only undertake forms of therapy that require 24-hour contact if the center has some provision for overnight hospitalization. Some therapeutic counseling, such as dealing with people who are depressives, might require some chemotherapy to be effective.

Where services or alternatives are very competitive, either because of limited resources or because of the logic of their goals, then having a centralized authority is very likely to lead to a hierarchy in choices. That is, some goals would receive very high priority and others very low priority. By contrast, where the authority structure is decentralized, then there is a much greater chance that each goal will receive equal weight, depending on the degree to which authority is decentralized.

The rationale for this hypothesis is obvious. In a single authority system, whoever captures the authority system is in a position to give priority to the goals they see as central. For instance, if the person who manages a community mental health center is a psychiatrist who believes strongly in traditional individual therapy, then programs which have chemotherapy, hospitalization, crisis intervention, and consultation and education might be slighted. But if a social worker runs the agency (or a psychiatrist who believes in preventive community mental health), then there may be a major stress on consultation and education with emphasis on coordinating with outside agencies. In short, depending on who becomes head and his or her vision of what is important, that particular goal will be stressed.

Where authority is decentralized, however, and each task is given its own organizational basis, then each has personnel and funds to fight for the survival of its task. For instance, if treatment of the aging has its own budget that the center

director has little power to alter radically and they have their
own personnel and facilities, then it is very likely that they
will stress aging regardless of who is appointed as head of the
overall center. But the extent to which such a decentralization
can take place must take into account the degree of interdependence with the other services and the nature of coordination
which replaces that of the strong executive. It means that the
autonomous units which are competitively related must have
some form of adjudication and unit confidentiality. Because
they have conflicting stresses, then any form of coordination
must take into account and have some procedures which
symbolically ends discussion rather than allowing the process
to lead to warfare that will tear the organization apart. This
form of adjudication could be a voting procedure, some form
of bringing in impartial arbitrators, some rules which assign
decisions on an equal basis so that no unit has more victories
than others and so forth. Insofar as the chief executives are
the impartial arbitrator, then they will have to be selected
(or replaced) in the same way that arbitrators ordinarily are
hired and fired. That is, their appointment and maintenance on
the job must be subject to approval by all units involved in the
competitive interdependence. If he is assumed to be partial to
one side or the other, then the offended unit should have the
power to have him removed. Where the subunits are highly
interdependent, and this is reflected in a high volume of exchange, then arbitrating disputes will be a full-time job and
may require more than one person. Where the volume of
exchange is small, then it might be part of other jobs.

It would be interesting to survey existing mental health
centers to see the extent to which they have decentralized
services and the extent to which such decentralization has led
to maintaining the tasks of the decentralized services. Alternatively, one must look at centralized services and see to what
extent they concentrate more specifically on given tasks and
have less diversity and the extent to which the task reflects
the orientation of the head of the organization. An additional
research issue to look at is centers which are decentralized, to

see the extent to which they have adjudication procedures and to see to what extent they are tied up in disruptive internal conflicts when they do not have such adjudication procedures.

An experimental study along these same lines and with specific reference to aging would ask some centers to set up a separate satellite organization of services for the aged, others to set up departments for the aged with personnel specifically hired for that purpose, while others set up specialized people, while still others be given a generalized mandate but no specialized personnel and to see to what extent services for the aged are stressed in each case and, what elements are lost because of the separation.

COORDINATION WITH OTHER COMMUNITY SERVICES

One of the chief problems facing people in aging and community mental health is the entire question of supporting services. Deinstitutionalization without supporting services (nursing homes) might be far worse than institutionalization with supporting services (state mental hospitals). Thus an extremely sensitive question is the extent to which one can have a community mental health program unless one has close coordination with various other services such as those providing supplementary housing, medicine, home nursing and leisure time facilities, transportation, and the like. These are obvious issues in the field of aging where the physical infirmities of the aged often make such needs for coordination extremely clear.

One of the key issues is the extent to which other services should be housed in the same building as the staff of the mental health center. There are at least three considerations which suggest close proximity. First, where the task to be coordinated involves much complexity, then generally face-to-face contact is required to communicate it adequately. Thus a therapist treating a client about to be evicted from a house with relatives might want to consult with a social worker about locating a new place with other relatives which may be more congenial to the mental state of the client. The discussion might involve great complexities of personality and trying to match this with various relatives or foster family possibilities.

Second, where the coordination involves issues of speed so that immediate decisions have to be made, or very resistant clients who will not go unless a staff member is present, it is generally better to have people within immediate walking distance. Finally, it would be argued that it is related to the degree of interdependence. If the coordination occurs very infrequently, then no matter what the advantages of proximity, it might not be worth it. However, if two services now consult frequently and are heavily intertwined over time then the two staffs will have to be very close.

Based on this analysis, one of the interesting studies would be one which systematically looks at community mental health centers to see if there is any variation in the extent to which they are located close to key services. How is this in turn related to the effectiveness of the service? Or the speed with which the community mental health center deliberately joins with the services most approximating the theoretical conditions mentioned above? If others retain their prior state of separation, what differences emerge?

Another key issue in coordinating services involves the extent to which coordination should be handled through a formal contract in which most contingencies are spelled out, or through coordinating agencies or committees where people have full-time appointments and a general mandate for coordination.

Generally, the factors which suggest formalized coordination are standardized elements to be exchanged and the volume of exchange to be undertaken. The more standardized the element, the easier it is to formalize the exchange. For instance, if two agencies are exchanging money, or names and addresses of clients, or the fixed allocation of time or space in the mass media, or the telephones and addresses of various agencies, then we are dealing with very standardized elements. It would be easy here to write a contract which took all contingencies into account. On the other hand, if two agencies are exchanging nonstandardized events where terminology is not common and where there are many contingencies, then it is difficult to write contracts that cover all contingencies.

A second factor which often leads to formalization is the volume of exchange. Where two agencies must exchange a great deal and staff cannot be expanded, then there is pressure to routinize tasks to achieve economies of large scale—the reason being that a nonroutinized task will require face to face contacts. With increasing volume this would put more pressure on the staff. Once tasks are routinized then they can be coordinated by rules, eliminating the need for people to do the coordination.

If these two factors are considered simultaneously then it could be argued that formal contracts which specify all contingencies should be undertaken where organizations have high volume of exchange and a highly standardized element to exchange. Where the organization must deal with nonstandardized material and it is an infrequent event, then face-to-face contact with no detailed agenda or fixed meeting schedule is optimal. Where the organization has high volume but it is a nonstandardized element that must be transmitted, then some specialized personnel must be involved to handle the volume. Some rules, but not all contingencies, can be specified in the rule because of the nonstandardized element. In such circumstances, a liaison committee or coordinating organization would have to be set up depending on the volume of exchange. On the other hand, where the organization has low volume, but a highly standardized exchange, then the organization might have rules; but because of the infrequency of the event, it might not find it profitable to make joint, mutually agreeable rules.

One interesting research project would be one which determined which type of linkage each community health center has with various agencies and to what extent they deviate from the predicted ideal and what, if any, difference that makes in the speed and accuracy of the coordination linkage. In general, if the linkage is more formal than the hypothesis suggests, then there should be complaints about the rigidity of the procedures, misapplication of rules or alternatively choke channels of communication to the top. The coordination should be slow or in error, as compared with organizations using more informal procedures. On the other hand, if the linkage is more informal than the ideal suggests, then the complaints should be that there are too many meetings that discuss the same matter over and over again and the lack of consistency of decision making. It should also be true that the coordination should be much slower than organizations using more formal linkages.

Alternatively, one can set up an experimental design asking community mental health centers to increase their linkages in terms of formality or informality as the theory suggests, and to see if indeed this increases the speed and accuracy of the exchange.

AWARENESS OF COORDINATION

Sometimes coordination takes place as a consequence of official organizational design. Thus the state mental hospital might have a very explicit and official procedure to coordinate with the community mental health center when they move people from the state hospital into the catchment area of the community mental health center. On the other hand the staff of the community mental health center might have a private agreement with a business concern to take so many of their clients into a working situation. Or the public might govern the nature of services offered by several agencies by virtue of their use of the market mechanisms to go to one agency rather than another for services. The question arises, when should coordination be part of the official program of the center? When should the staff handle it privately but not as an official part of their job? And when should it be the concern of the larger public? Where the organization officially designates coordi-

nation as part of the job, it reduces uncertainty, while the staff
engaged in private forms of coordination increases uncertainty.
The reason being that, in private forms of coordination, if anything goes wrong the staff must bear the burden without
organizational support; e.g., they may be fired. In addition, the
organization will shift personnel without considering the needs
of coordination, and the individuals undertaking the coordination can drop out whenever it suits their whims This means that
people undertaking private forms of coordination must know
and trust each other if coordination is to continue. Where trust
cannot be established, using staff without officially designating
coordination would be less than ideal.

Why encourage private rather than offical endorsements of
coordination? One case would be situations where organizations are officially not permitted to coordinate because it
would violate some of their other goals. For instance, it might
be a good thing if schools and churches provided a program for
the elderly returning to the community. The goals of the larger
society, however, might suggest that church and school should
be kept separate. Rather than seeking an official exception to
this larger social norm, it might be better in specific ad hoc
situations to develop a private staff type of coordination. Yet
another situation may occur where the staff may feel that locating a client with mental health problems in a job would be a
good thing. They would require, however, special considerations initially on the matter of absenteeism and the ability to
take orders which might violate company and union agreements. It is also bad for them to be publicly labeled mental
health cases. For these reasons the staff of the mental health
center may seek private agreements with the business and
union rather than seek an official endorsement. Such informal
coordination is also necessary when there is no time to set up
official coordination.

There are two reasons for the demand that the public be the
source of coordination through a device such as a market
mechanism. First, it occurs in situations where the getting

together of the formal organization might be bad for the client. Thus if only one agency controlled all therapy, or if there were a highly coordinated group who assigned clients to given agencies, then the staff would be more likely to take their own convenience into account rather than client interests. But where there are many agencies who do not coordinate, then the client would be free to choose and thus force the agency to pay attention to the client's needs. Some have suggested a voucher program which gives the clients discretion about which agency they will choose. This assumes that the clients can judge which agencies are meeting their needs, and can select some kind of highly standardized market mechanism such as a price or voucher system.

A second reason for using the public rather than agencies applies when neither staff nor private agencies can coordinate. In classical economic theory this would occur if there were too many agencies for coordination. The same situation can arise, however, when agencies lack resources, and extensive conflict among them might prevent official coordination or private staff negotiations. In such cases, coordination would have to take place through the public.

The obvious situation where public mechanisms are rejected is where it is felt that there is either an uneven distribution of money or knowledge in the population meaning that only certain segments of the population will receive services if a market mechanism is used. In this regard, market mechanisms are inoperable when the consumer cannot assess the outcome. Thus consumers are often unable to determine if their doctor is good or not. Under such circumstances, the freedom to choose doctors under a price mechanism may not really serve the client's needs. For price mechanisms to work would require an institution of advocate experts to whom the clients would turn for technical advice. More research in assessing when officially sanctioned private staff arrangements and when public modes of coordination are best, would be very useful. Some of the crucial assumptions regarding the community's

ability to assess its services will be developed later on community participation in mental health centers. The research
issues are not developed here any further except to suggest
that, when a high degree of official awareness is joined with
considerations of standardization and volume, it is possible to
discriminate among many different ideal coordination mechanisms (for instance, when coordination between agencies involves low volume, e.g., few people, nonstandardized elements
are being exchanged, or trying to set policy for coordination,
and where the matter is unofficial, or the head of agency does
not approve, then the use of a social occasion like lunch or a
party may be a good occasion to coordinate). If this were official, then ad hoc interstaff conferences with no fixed agenda
would be ideal.

The problems of coordination of services are complex. They
involve questions of how organizations might best coordinate
when they have many contradictory linkages (e.g., which ones
should one choose or are there procedures for isolating the
linkages from each other). They also involve prior considerations about whether interdependence is facilitative or competitive. Should the coordinating procedures, then, involve
adjudication or some kind of scientific consensual decision-
making? There is also the problem of balancing the needs of the
organization for autonomy with the needs for coordination.
This means there must be some procedures for maintaining
distance as well as for coordination if there is no desire to have
coordination produce a merger. How does one, simultaneously, stress boundaries and distance between organizations
while, at the same time, ask organizations to exchange?

There is one issue regarding coordination that has been
stressed by others and that is the extent to which the very
structure of the organization affects coordination with others.
Community mental health centers must coordinate with other
organizations that, comparatively speaking, are more hier-
archical, rules-oriented, impersonal, and have more delimited and specialized tasks (such as Social Security offices,

income maintenance divisions of welfare, various governmental licensing bureaus, police, and so forth. The more rules-
oriented the structure, the less able the organization is to coordinate nonstandardized elements with another agency. For
rules-oriented structures to deal with nonstandardized tasks,
generally means that the person on the top must handle the
matter personally. If the exchanges are frequent, the person on
top is quickly overwhelmed or has to delegate to his staff to the
point where the structure of the organization is changed.
Where the organization is professional and collegial then they
have a problem in dealing with coordination involving standardized procedures such as filling out forms or keeping attendance records but are very good at dealing with nonstandardized
events. As a consequence, when two organizations with
radically different structures have to coordinate their activities, they find themselves in conflict more because of the structure of their organization than the specific goals requiring
coordination. Thus, a therapy center dealing with people seeking vocational retraining because of mental illness, might be
required by a welfare center supplying training funds to provide daily attendance records as evidence that the client was
indeed in vocational retraining. But the therapy might be such
that the client might legitimately be absent from his therapist
for long stretches of time, and, from the point of view of the
therapist, such a request seems meaningless paper work which
they neglect to do. The welfare department, required by law to
account for its funds and to ensure there is no fraud, might have
a staff trained to avoid procedures that provide individuals
with discretion. They, therefore, insist on a highly routinized
form of coordination. How does one coordinate best where
one has organizational structures which push people into
different linkages? Again, this is a research question which has
been elaborated in terms of ideal solutions.

DEGREE OF INSTITUTIONALIZATION

There are yet other questions which will be mentioned but not developed in this chapter. They involve considering the entire mental health system and the role of the community centers within that system. Many practitioners now readily acknowledge that there is indeed room for closed institutions such as state hospitals for handling some types of clients. In addition, they agree that there is room for more decentralized institutions, such as half-way houses or even group homes, as well as the ultimate in decentralization in the use of natural support systems and community mental health centers. What has to be examined far more systematically, is the kind of client who might ideally be serviced by each system; no one solution is best for all clients. Even if one solution would be ideal, it would be wise (given the fact that many disagree), to test this assumption by comparative study.

There are, again, two research designs which should be considered. One would study people serviced and not serviced in each of these facilities and try to assess which clients seem to be serviced best by which procedure. The other would differentiate types of clients faced by community mental health programs. These types range from the senile elderly who can no longer control their bodily functions, to those with some strong mental impairments but who can manage many of the everyday tasks of living—if supervised. If one can set up a list of such clients a priori, and the clients can be assigned to the various settings so that each setting has some clients, then one can determine systematically which is ideal. An alternative procedure would search out a setting treating the range of clients and without experimental design, trying to see which setting is best.

A central problem in this regard is the continuing role of the natural support systems at every stage of institutionalization. Several studies suggest that where nursing home residents have continuing contact with their outside kin and friends, they are given better care by the staff. The problem of how such contacts between kin groups with their stress on positive affect and nepotistic ties can be coordinated with the institution with its needs for routinization, delimited commitment, and merit, is very similar to that discussed earlier with regard to the mental health centers and the community. But, the problems are more severe when dealing with completely institutionalized clients because institutionalized care has such a radically different structure from the kinship system. This situation lends itself to experimentation. For instance, state institutions could encourage kin participation with residents by providing free parking and lengthening visiting hours. They could be located near major population centers, provide rooms where people can meet, encourage kin to volunteer for tasks within the institution and, in turn, encourage residents to visit kin. Such systematic variations can be examined to determine the consequences for clients.

COMMUNITY ROLE IN CENTERS

Community mental health center policy involves not only technical knowledge but rather basic value priorities. Community members might be as well versed as the staff, and should play a major role if the center is indeed to serve the interests of the community. In addition, community participation can check a staff gone wild—that is, a staff more concerned with meeting staff needs than client needs. This check can be direct where the acts of the staff involve nontechnical matters, and it can be indirect through advocate outside experts brought in by community members to check the technical work of the staff. Finally, the community can be brought in by the staff to help those clients who require nontechnical aid (such as cooking, chauffeuring, providing companionship, and the like). This was covered in our prior section. In this section we want to deal with the needs of the center and community members as guardians of community interests.

In this regard there are several issues. First, the staff and community might not agree on what constitutes value decisions and what constitutes technical decisions. Therapists might not see that the choice between types of individual therapy contains many value components where the community members can and should play an important role. Staff members with a vested job interest might see their activity as crucial and the decision as completely technical. Where the technical and nontechnical aspects are closely interwoven, there may be a great temptation on the part of the staff to use the technical aspects to cover up the nontechnical ones. A second problem revolves around community access to decision-making processes. There may be or may not be institutional avenues through which community members can participate in such decisions. Do centers have lay boards consisting of community members being served? If so, what decisions are brought before them? And which are ignored?

Thus far, two areas of research are indicated: one that determines which areas professionals typically see as nontechnical and which they see as technical and what would be their attitude to community participation in various areas that some "objective" judges say is nontechnical, regardless of staff's view. Related to this would be studies of the mechanisms of introducing change in staff perception and in areas where it is difficult to determine whether the task was technical or not. What would be the mechanisms of resolving such disputes?

A second kind of research would look at various community mental health centers to determine how easy (or difficult) it is for community members to participate as policy makers. To what extent does the center have a board of directors consisting of community lay people and to what extent are there no real provisions for such a board?

A related issue is the question of who that board represents. Does it represent a wealthy elite or a group who have the same interests as the staff? Or does it represent the clients who are being directly served by the staff? To what extent do the client or client groups have an organization which exists autonomously from the community mental health centers? For instance, in many of the Office of Economic Opportunity (OEO) programs, there was a mandate that the poor be included in community boards. Where the board was mixed, however, it was often the case that those groups which had autonomous organizations outside the boards could maintain themselves much better than those who were only board members. What sometimes happened in the latter case was that when an individual was defeated on the board, that would be the end of his position, while in the former case, the outside organization could sustain a point of view even when a given member was defeated. Equally important, where the community members felt that the problem arose because of staff technical incompetency, they often could not make a clear judgment because of their own lack of expertise. Where the community has some form of outside organization then they generally have the resources to hire or borrow an outside expert to make such a judgment. There are two illustrations of this. In the case of mental retardation, there are parent groups who have organized and play such a role vis-à-vis the developing of legislation and the monitoring of institutions for the retarded. In the case of the elderly, there are two types of autonomous groups —one such as the Gray Panthers and one of kin groups organized to serve elderly parents often too ill to look after themselves.

Thus, one of the studies that we should like to see is one that compares community mental health centers as follows: a center with no community board or a weak one staffed by people selected by the professional staff or in sympathy with them; a community board with significant client members or people with common interests such as kin; and a community mental health center having the latter but, in addition, where the clients or their kin have an autonomous outside organization.

The research task would be to determine the differing problems, if any, that staff emphasized where community members
had strong and weak input, and to what extent clients do
better or worse under various conditions of community participation. Major aspects to look for would be new client priorities
superceding staff's convenience, the problems of client groups
introducing issues of nepotism or lower standards into the
center, and the extent to which greater and more fruitful use of
natural support systems is undertaken. Community conflicts
might be heightened where the community consists of different
populations with different value systems emphasizing different
courses of action. If there is no mechanism for settling differences, conflict could impair the effectiveness of the center.

This problem lends itself to experimental design. In one
study group, the elderly and their kin could be organized to
have a self-sustaining, independent organization plus a place
on the community mental health center board; another group
could be given board membership only; and a third group
would not be given membership. One would determine to what
extent: (1) the interests of the aged were emphasized at centers;
(2) staff abuse to the aged was lessened; and (3) abuse was
punished when it occurred.

A research issue arises because new legislation mandates
that community mental health centers be of service to the aged.
A set of studies can be immediately undertaken to see how this
legislative mandate is, in fact, implemented. Part of this can be
considered an evaluation study, and part can be considered an
effort to locate the mechanics of introducing change into an
organization. To some extent, many of the prior considerations mentioned above bear on the question of introducing
change within an organization. Thus, the idea of putting older
people or their kin on the community board has some implications for the degree to which change in emphasis on the aged
will be implemented. In many cases the most powerful incentive for change within an organization occurs because of
forces outside an organization. Therefore, to understand pro-

cedures for changes one must often have an understanding of the extent to which powerful forces outside an organization seek change and what the mechanisms are that they have for intervening within the organization, some of the key issues involve staff resistance or agreement to change. Another important element is the degree of complexity of the change. For instance, a change in opening and closing hours for the mental health center can be a fairly simple, noncomplex change. We are speaking about a clearly observable phenomenon which can be assessed in a standardized way. By contrast, a more complex form of change is that which requires services to the aged as a major service of the mental health centers. In this case, change might mean basic and different forms of treatment procedures. For some therapists, it might mean a change in orientation if they believe that treatment of the elderly for neurosis or psychosis is not possible. With such highly nonstandardized forms of change, it is necessary not only to have a mandate but also a complex set of training procedures and some processes for assessing whether or not the staff agrees with—and implements—the basic policy. If the staff is in disagreement, one must be able to take one of several steps to ensure that the change is implemented. They are either to fire staff who are not willing to implement the changes, or hire new staff whose basic values agree with the new policy, or have intensive retraining to resocialize staff into the new policy positions. When such actions are not possible, it is unlikely that the changes will be effectively implemented. Attempts to change prison and hospital staffs from a custodial to a treatment orientation would provide investigators with some good analogies.

What should be understood, (even where the staff is positively oriented to change) is that very little will be accomplished in dealing with complex changes that require decentralized staff operations unless there is provision for substantial apprenticeship procedures for training them in the new procedures. If therapy for the aged is a highly specialized field, then the staff of mental health centers requires extensive re-training or new staff must be brought in if change is to be implemented.

Complex changes can be introduced most quickly and successfully where staff has values and training in accord with the change, and all that is required is a simple statement of the new goals and minor forms of apprenticeship training. Alternatively, quick changes of the complex decentralized kinds can be undertaken where one has the ability to hire new staff with the proper orientation and training and to locate them in situations where they will be protected from other staff or to be able to fire the old staff simultaneously. Where staff are opposed or do not have the requisite training, then change will require freedom to hire and fire or funds for extensive apprenticeship training and, in some cases, professional resocialization.

By contrast, where the change involves simple or highly standardized and easily observable phenomena such as the hours that centers are open or the simple fact that services, such as crisis centers, are in existence without question as to how they are being implemented, then they can be implemented by simple directives or factual cognitive forms of training and threats to withhold funds or firing people.

These same threats, when applied to the more complex forms of change, will lead to the phenomenon of changes which meet the letter but not the spirit. One will have people designated to deal with the aged, but the therapy processes will be inadequate. One will have statistics which show that the aged are contacted but mostly by referral and with little serious intent. One will be a direct service which does not really do much for the aged or deals with only that group of the aged that can be dealt with by traditional therapy.

What is suggested is a series of experimental studies to assess the degree of complexity of the change which one is seeking to introduce, the extent to which the staff is sympathetic and, in addition, has the requisite technical tools. In situations where the staff is highly resistent or lacks technical tools, the change effort will be accompanied by heavy apprenticeship training, as well as an effort to resocialize outlooks toward retraining the aged. By contrast, where the staff is sympathetic and has the requisite training, a very modest form of retraining and simple policy directives will be undertaken. These two groups will be compared with matched groups for which simple policy directives will be sent down, with training handled in lectures rather than in an apprenticeship and where threats to withhold funds would be made if changes were not made. The prediction will be that both the former types will do equally well but that both the latter types will fail to implement change. A more complex design would take into account more standardized changes, such as demands that centers be open in retirement villages. Given the same set of stimuli, the opposite prediction would be made.

Again, some basic elements have been outlined that should be included in such studies. The actual design would involve many more complexities.

MORE GENERAL CONSIDERATIONS
OF RESEARCH

In addition to the above research, there is a need for some, more general, types of research that cover all the above problems simultaneously or that deal with central methodological considerations.

What would be enormously useful at this point (and a fundamental backdrop to many of the above studies) would be a census study which indicates the distribution of various forms of stresses and strains as well as mental problems of the aged in the population as a whole. This, in turn, should be matched to a similar census study of community mental health centers to see what kinds of people they are treating and the nature of their illnesses. We have only the crudest indicators, (e.g., the fact that in some centers the percentage of aged is only 1% of the clients, while the population of the aged in general is closer to 10%) telling us that something is wrong. If the aged have a higher incidence of mental ill health, then they should have a higher percentage of treatment than their 10%. If they have a lower incidence, then they should have a lower percentage. Furthermore, we do not know who among the aged is being treated and for what. Are we dealing mostly with the robust aged or those with strong natural support systems or the frail isolated or those with weak support systems? Are we dealing with the aged who are fearful or not fearful of being designated as mentally ill? Are we dealing with staff which see the aged as low priority in contrast with the young? Or a staff which feels that there are no good techniques for dealing with the aged? Or a staff which is sympathetic but so overworked that they only respond to those clients who are most demanding? The more precise statement of who is being treated and the analysis of staff characteristics would be of great value in planning programs of change.

To do many of these studies, it is important to develop reliable and valid instruments. One of the key problems of research is that of differentiating error introduced by the nature of the instruments from meaningful findings. Thus it is often very difficult to decide, when investigators come up with different findings on the same issue whether the findings are indeed different, or are but a function of using different or unreliable instruments. In this regard, the work of the Older Americans Resources and Services Program (OARS) at Duke University must indeed be encouraged. But when working with instruments intended for practitioners as part of their assessment or diagnostic procedures, there are two additional developments which are essential, and where the OARS type of work must be expanded. First, it is not enough to have instruments which relate in a statistically significant manner to an outside criterion of validity or in some measure of reliability. What also must be shown is that the association is sufficiently high to be meaningful to the practitioner. Pearson correlates of .02 could be statistically significant but of no real practical use to mental health staff. What is even more central is that correlations which are very high for purposes of basic research might be very low for practitioners. Correlations of .50 or .80 which would be definitive for basic research, explain only .25 and .64% of the variance. For many practitioners they may be far too low to depend on for their goals.

Perhaps even more important than the need to assess the height of the relation is the need to understand the nature of errors of the measure. There are generally two kinds of errors that measures can make. One is the error of saying that something is true which is not true, and the second is the error of saying something is false which is, in fact, true. For instance, in setting up an instrument to assess mental health, the instrument may err by saying some people are sick who, in fact, are well, or by saying some people are well who are, in fact, sick. For many purposes these two errors are not equal. A measure can be far better in eliminating one type of error than the other. If one is more important than another, it is possible to use the instrument even if it has low overall associations, because the lack of correlation comes from the type of error one does not care about.

For instance, an instrument may almost never make the error classifying people as well when they are, in fact, sick. However, it may, in 70% of the cases, label well people as sick. Such a measure may be a good screening device for a doctor even when it accurately handles only part of his cases; the doctor would only have to look at that segment of his cases, (those labeled sick), and accept the instrument's diagnosis for all those labeled well. If he did not have the measure he would have to look at all the cases. But if policy makers wanted to use this same test without the doctor's interview, then it may be viewed as a bad instrument.

Therefore, it is very important in developing these standardized instruments that are going to be used for any policy or practical purpose to have some understanding of what types of error they are likely to involve and what the consequences for the practitioner are of committing these errors.

In addition to such considerations, instruments like the OARS must be much more sophisticated in terms of the natural support systems, the nature of organizational structure and community access to social services, as well as staff motivations. Having said this, it should be clearly understood that these are directions for further improvement. But one must use what one has, and in this regard the OARS instrument should be seriously considered when one engages in the census research suggested above.

Much federal legislation includes funds and a mandate to conduct evaluation studies of programs. At the same time, there is a strong feeling that such evaluation is not done—or done with the letter of the law but not the spirit. What can be done about this? To some extent, the discussion on organizational change bears directly on this issue. But, because of the legislative mandates and fund allotments, it may be important specifically to highlight problems in the two types of evaluation. The first is one meant to help practitioners improve their daily work and which is not being used to judge them as good or bad. These are records that may go only to the person being evaluated. In contrast, there are evaluation procedures which assess the success of a practice or program and advise dropping them or radically changing them if they are unsuccessful.

The former evaluation, if it has failed, has failed because establishing the criteria of success and failure are not easy, and, where possible, implementing changes may require far more resources and training than most organizations are prepared to handle. In other words, if it is a complex change, then the staff must be given long-term apprenticeship training in its use. Second, where staff are resistant to such implementations because in principle, they feel such quantitative evaluations are bad or involve too much work or overcommitment of resources, then any change will require, in addition to the evaluation, some fundamental resocialization. In some instances, additional resources will be needed to make use of the new procedures.

With regard to the problem of evaluating programs and people to determine merit, another major problem arises: the need to protect one's livelihood. It is the rare individual who can view such an evaluation dispassionately. It is also true because of the nature of the instruments used (often very much in dispute) and the nature of evaluation procedures, that those people evaluated negatively often do not accept the assessments. As a consequence, those feeling comfortable about what they are doing might find evaluation especially threatening, and might either discourage it or do it as a political facade (that is, ensure that the evaluation will always be favorable). This is accomplished by controlling the evaluators and the evaluators picking and choosing material which is favorable to the agency. This then raises the entire question of the autonomy of the evaluators.

Many complex issues of therapy are not easily measured. Where evaluators rely only on quantitative measures that have low levels of reliability then there is no way in principle that one can come up with findings which show that the program has affected large numbers of people in a substantial way. For instance, an instrument that has a reliability of .50 (and where one assumes that the error is randomly distributed) is unlikely to come up with a finding that a program's efforts are correlated more than .50 with its goals. Where one has to use several such instruments simultaneously to explain program effects, the probability rapidly goes against being able to demonstrate that programs have any substantial effect. Therefore, it is very important in doing such program evaluation that the measure used be as close as possible to the actual outcomes one wants to assess. For instance, if it is the mental health of the patients one is seeking to assess, then reliance should not solely be put on tests like the OARS because they will systematically underestimate effects. Therefore, in addition, there should be some mental health experts, such as psychiatrists, who actually per-

form before and after assessments of the elderly to see if there
has been some improvement or measures which directly show
the elderly functioning better in the community than they did
before treatment.

It is clear that this chapter has only touched on issues, and
has left many questions unanswered. The intention has been to
highlight some of the key areas and to outline the variables that
should be looked at. The intent was to sensitize researchers to
the key problems of research in the delivery of service and hope
they will, in turn, elaborate and develop the more complete set
of variables necessary for the actual undertaking of research.

6

THE INFORMAL SUPPORT SYSTEM:
ITS RELEVANCE IN THE
LIVES OF THE ELDERLY

Marjorie H. Cantor

An important theme about the person in most cultures centers on the balance of dependency and independency needs. Many traditional values concern the ability of the individual to survive and prosper with a minimum of assistance from those around. This ethos of independence and self-sufficiency still permeates our culture and is still a standard against which individuals and groups often measure their own and each other's worth.

From the life cycle perspective there are two significant stages in which the culture more often accepts dependency needs—at the beginning and at the end. It is therefore considered appropriate for infants and children to be nurtured by parents and significant others as they are socialized into the culture. But even within this nurture, the emphasis is on independence and self-mastery. And, again, as persons grow older and more frail society looks with greater tolerance on their needs for assistance and support. In the case of old age, however, as the balance shifts from independence to dependence, the potential for normative conflicts increases. Thus, an older person is caught in a dilemma: adherence to deeply rooted cultural norms of self-sufficiency and independence characteristic of adult years on the one hand, and concrete needs for assistance on the other, as health, physical strength, mobility, and other economic resources decline.

How can such conflicting values be resolved with the greatest dignity for older people? Who is most appropriately seen as the preferred avenue of assistance if and when an older person is faced with the need for it? Do different kinds of tasks and differing stages of aging require differing modalities of intervention? A clear understanding of the modern kinship structure and the relation of the informal support network to formal organizations is essential if persons working with older people are to play a positive role in helping the elderly resolve the dependency crisis of old age.

First, and most important, is the notion supported by current research (our own as well as that of others): older people perceive the informal network of kin (particularly children), friends, and neighbors as the most appropriate source of social support in most situations of need. Not only is the informal system so seen, but it is to this network that older people turn first and most frequently. Only when assistance from the informal system is unavailable or kin and significant others can no longer absorb the burden of support (either because of the excessive time or money commitment involved or because of lack of requisite skill or technical know-how), do older people and their families turn to formal organizations. This reliance on the informal system, however, in no way negates the acceptance by the elderly and their families of the role of government and other formal organizations in the provisions of broad-based economic, health, housing, educational, safety, and transportation entitlements. Rather, it is through sharing tasks between formal organizations and primary groups that the well-being of older people will be most advanced. Thus, the social support system of older people can best be seen as an amalgam of kin, friend, neighbor, and societal services, each having different roles and differing relative importance at various phases in the aging process. But the underlying goal of any support system, be it formal or informal, is to strengthen an older person's sense of mastery over self and environment.

THE SOCIAL SUPPORT SYSTEM OF
OLDER PEOPLE

Before discussing the role of the informal network in providing assistance to older people, it would be well to examine the notion of social support system and its functions. A social support system is a pattern of continuous or intermittent ties and interchanges of mutual assistance that plays a significant role in maintaining the psychological, social, and physical integrity of the individual over time. For it to function, consistency and availability of relations or resources are required to meet a variety of needs whether ongoing or time-limited. Included in the definition are both informal and formal activities as well as the personal support services that enable older people to remain independent. A social support system enables older people to fulfill three needs: socialization; carrying out the tasks of daily living; and personal assistance during times of crisis.

Within this broad rubric are found both formal and informal components or subsystems. The informal support network is distinguishable from the formal or organizational by its individualistic and nonbureaucratic nature, and by the fact that its members are selected by the elderly from among kin, friends, and neighbors. This selection entails considerations of affect as well as efficiency, and is influenced by social class and ethnicity.

SOCIAL SUPPORT
SYSTEMS—A NETWORK APPROACH

Inasmuch as the social support system of an older person is best characterized as having both formal and informal components, any attempt to understand its operation requires a careful study of both individual and institutional forces and their interactive effect. If one can envision an older person at the core of, and interacting with, a series of subsystems which usually operate independently but at times intersect, the definition of a broad-based social support system becomes clearer.

At the outermost reaches are the political and economic entities which determine the basic entitlements available to all older people; these significantly affect their well-being in income maintenance, health, housing, safety, education, and transportation. Somewhat closer to the older person in social distance, though still far from playing a central role, are the governmental and voluntary agencies who carry out economic and social policies by providing the actual services mandated under laws such as the Older Americans Act, Social Security, Medicare, and the like. These organizations, in the two outer rings, are clearly the formal part of the system. Like all bureaucratic organizations they attempt to function instrumentally and objectively according to an ideology of efficiency and rationality.

Still closer, and standing somewhere between formal organizations and primary group members, are nonservice, formal or quasi-formal organizations (or their representatives). These also can perform a helping function with respect to the elderly in the role of postman, shopkeeper, bartender, building superintendent, and friendship delegations from unions or churches. This network is tertiary inasmuch as it resembles the informal network but springs from, and is related to, formal organizations.

And finally, closest to the daily life of an older person are the individuals who compose the informal support system—

kin, friends, and neighbors. It is precisely these significant others with whom older people have the most frequent interaction, both instrumentally and affectively, and who compose the broad basis of the social support system in the United States.

THE INFORMAL SUPPORT SYSTEM IN THE INNER CITY OF NEW YORK

Recent investigations in New York City and elsewhere by Cantor, Shanas, Sussman, Brody, Sherwood, and Litwak, have been aimed at documenting the role of children, friends, neighbors in the lives of older people and drawing from such data the social policy and practice implications for formal organizations, particularly governmental and social agencies.

In 1970, the New York City Department for the Aging undertook probably the largest cross-cultural study of the lives and needs of older people living in a central city. This study, *The Elderly in the Inner City* (Cantor et al., 1970), had a probability sample of 1,552 persons highly representative of the over 400,000 elderly living in the 26 inner city neighborhoods. It should be noted that in New York there is no central or core city as such, and inner city conditions are found in all five boroughs. But the 26 study neighborhoods had all the classic symptoms of central cities—high incidence of welfare case loads, high infant mortality, deteriorated environmental conditions, and so forth. They clearly duplicated the objective conditions found in the central cities of other urban centers in the United States. In this way, the findings apply to other parts of the country as well.

Respondents were interviewed for one hour in their own homes and in their own languages (where appropriate). The sample was evenly divided along the age continuum, ranging from 60 to 75+; 49.9% of the respondents were white, 37.9% black, and 13.9% Hispanic. Although the sample was weighted toward the poorer elderly, there was considerable socioeconomic spread because in the inner city neighborhoods of New York City, are found many lower- and middle-class whites who are long-time residents of the area. There were, however, few really affluent elderly among the respondents. Thus, the important variables of ethnicity and class were built into the study from the start. The findings give important clues concerning the role of family, friends, and neighbors, in helping urban elderly to maintain their independent status in the community.

FAMILY AND OTHER KIN

In analyzing the informal support available to older people, three distinct parts are identifiable, each with a different role to play: children and other kin, close friends or intimates, and neighbors. Most important in quantity and types of assistance are children, particularly in situations where there is no spouse in the home.

Contrary to myths that circulate widely about today's parent-child relationships, the study findings indicate that most inner city elderly have children, and they have not been abandoned by their children. Familial bonds are strong and there is evidence of mutual affection and assistance between generations. Thus, children provide parents with a significant amount of assistance at times of crisis, help out with gifts, money, and provide help with the tasks of daily living. They are also an important source of emotional support and companionship.

Moreover, there is substantial reciprocity between generations—the flow of assistance is not one-way. Parents, in turn, help children when there is an illness in the family, provide child care, give gifts, and, to a lesser extent, give advice about child rearing and major family decisions. The amount of help parents receive from children is related to the age of the older person and the paucity of income, suggesting that as older people become more vulnerable, their children respond with more of the needed assistance.

In summary, with respect to the role of children, it would appear that siblings and other relatives, although valuable in the absence of spouse and children, play a less-important social support role. This is undoubtably influenced by their own conditions of age and frailty.

FRIENDS AND NEIGHBORS

Although most older people have one or more offspring as the foundation of an informal support system, there are many who have no children (approximately one-third in the New York City sample), and others have children living far away. For such older persons, close friends and particularly neighbors can, and indeed, do, compensate as primary social supports.

But, even if older people receive weekly or bi-weekly visits from children, this hardly satisfies their needs for socialization and intimacy on a day-to-day basis. Thus, friends and neighbors become important secondary support elements to those with children, and the amount of their assistance is often crucial in whether or not an older person turns for help to the formal social support system of government or voluntary agencies.

As persons age there is an increased tendency to be neighborhood-bound, and interaction with friends outside of the area diminishes. Persons designated as friends usually live in the neighborhood, and the distinction between friends and neighbors is blurred.

Most elderly live in age-integrated neighborhoods (and, in urban areas, age integrated-apartment buildings), and the majority of their neighbors may be younger. This does not appear, however, to preclude the development of mutual patterns of assistance between elderly and those around them. In fact, a striking feature of the neighbor-elderly relationship in the inner city neighborhoods of New York is the high degree of reciprocity.

Neighbor-friends and the elderly not only shop for each other and help out in emergencies, but neighbors accompany older people to the doctor, the Social Security office, and may on occasion bank for them. The most frequent form of assistance, however, is help during emergencies. The very proximity of neighbors makes them particularly important to older people in crisis situations involving illness, crime, fire, and so forth. In most cases, assistance from neighbors during illness is either short-term or sporadic, with the longer-range care of the more seriously or chronically ill generally assumed by kin. But, because neighbor-friends often play an important compensatory role with respect to elders without kin, in such cases it is not uncommon for a neighbor to assume more long-range responsibilities during illness, sometimes involving crucial decision-making with regard to hospitalization or home care. The degree of involvement of a neighbor-friend at times of illness, or in the chores of daily living, is therefore not only a function of the intimacy of the relationship and the nature of the task, but is heavily influenced by the presence or absence of kin.

Although substantial levels of help are forthcoming from neighbors and friends with respect to crisis intervention and chores of daily living, it is in the areas of socialization and tension reduction that the network of neighbor-friends is most significant for the elderly. Particularly in urban areas, the importance of the neighborhood as a socialization center cannot be underestimated. The steady interaction occurring with neighbors-friends not only offers a way of using time, but is a principal avenue in the case of many elderly for ego testing and reaffirmation of personal worth.

Visiting, sitting and talking, and eating with neighbors are some of the many social support tasks assumed under the rubric of socialization. They are essential to sound mental health and must frequently be carried out on a day-to-day basis by friends and neighbors.

EFFECT OF CULTURE AND CLASS

To what extent do class and ethnicity influence the nature and operation of the system? The New York City urban findings indicate that these are major dimensions, particularly in urban areas with a highly heterogenous population. Using a multivariate analysis (thereby controlling for other variables such as sex, social class, income, and level of functional ability), it was found that being Hispanic made a considerable difference in the nature of the system. There were, however, few significant differences between the white and black respondents. Thus, the Hispanic elderly were found consistently to have a greater potential for support from children than whites or blacks and a higher level of interaction with children. Hispanic elderly receive more help from children, give more in return, and are significantly closer to their children. This substantiates the study hypothesis regarding the positive effects of the informal support network still being part of an extended family system. What was surprising, given the evidence of an extensive system of mutual interdependency between generations in the black community, was the absence of a similar heightened interaction with children in the case of the elderly blacks in the sample. The lack of significant differences in kinship support patterns between black and white respondents should not, however, be seen as the absence of mutual assistance between parents and children in the black community. Rather, it is a testimony to the often overlooked high level of interaction which is still occurring between white elderly and their children.

But even more important than ethnicity as a predictive factor was the independent contribution made by the social class of the respondent. Thus, the higher the social class, the less involved the relationship between parents and children. As social class rises, the number of children decreases, as does the likelihood of having at least one such child, the frequency of interaction, and the amount of help given and received.

It would appear that as social class rises, nuclear families in a kinship network maintain a greater distance between themselves, and that elderly parents are less intently involved on a day-to-day basis with their adult children. But the higher socioeconomic status elderly are not forsaken by children. Rather, assistance and intervention is considered appropriate and is, in fact, given in times of crisis, but socialization with peers, rather than children, is expected to fill the void of intensive parent-child interaction.

An examination of the data on friendship interactions, bears out these expectations. Thus, as social class rises, the respondents are likely to have a wider circle of functional friends or intimates. With respect to neighbors, ethnicity is a significant variable in the case of the blacks—they are more likely than whites or Hispanic elderly to have a greater number of functional neighbors, to receive from and give more help to their neighbors and to do more things together with neighbors. Other researchers in the black community have pointed out that alliances are commonly formed between kin and friends who help one another and that friendships are formed in the idiom of kinship. The findings of *The Elderly in the Inner City* would appear to bear this out. The foregoing suggests the great complexity involved in analyzing or predicting the operation of the informal support system in any given situation. Thus, which primary group is called on or activated in given situations of need by an older person is a function of several factors that operate either separately or most probably in conjunction with each other. Nature of the task to be performed is one factor, but probably more important as a determinant is the value system and cultural orientation of the older person regarding the nature of kin relationships and the performance of appropriate roles, particularly by children. And most important in determining the patterns of assistance is the social class factor, particularly in the future, as more highly acculturated cohorts of elderly emerge.

THE INTERFACE OF FORMAL AND INFORMAL NETWORKS

Two important questions remain to be considered: Do older people have a preference with regard to appropriate support givers? And what is the nature of the interface between the formal and informal networks at different stages of aging?

The support system of the elderly is composed of the following elements—spouse, children, siblings and other relatives, friends, neighbors and formal organizations. The Inner City questionnaire, in addition to behavioral questions, included a series of normative questions aimed at eliciting the preferred social support element in ten hypothetical, critical incidents. The ten situations presented included instrumental tasks in the areas of health, finance, and tasks of daily living and examples of effective assistance. The choices ranged from no one (myself) through the various primary groups to formal organizations. Analysis of the responses suggests the existence of a hierarchical-compensatory model regarding the choice of support givers with close kin, principally spouse or child, seen as the primary and most appropriate source of assistance regardless of task. Only to the extent that family, particularly children, are not available, or in the case of certain well defined roles, do friends, neighbors, and formal organizations become important in providing social supports.

Thus, for example, in the area of socialization, and day-to-day companionship, friends and neighbors play a significant role. Likewise, friends and neighbors are helpful for short-term emergency assistance such as summoning the doctor, police, or child, or for shopping in inclement weather. But the most extensive use of friends and neighbors appears to occur in a compensatory manner when kin, and particularly children, are either nonexistent or nonfunctional.

If the informal support system is hierarchical-compensatory, does it vary according to the level of functional ability of the older person; specifically, the well and independent, the comparatively well, those needing services to prevent institutionalization, and those requiring institutionalization or congregate living?

The social support system of older people is a continuum with an amalgam of kin, friend, neighbor, and societal services, each having different relative importance in various phases of aging. Although most communities have agencies ready to provide assistance, turning to such agencies is far from the first reaction of most people, including the elderly. Older Americans are fiercely independent and desirous of managing on their own or, if necessary, turning to those with whom they have a primary relationship such as a child or neighbor. Thus, the agencies that comprise the formal support elements are mainly used as older persons become more frail and less able to carry out the chores of daily living; or as personal or family resources are strained or become nonexistent; or as required in the case of culturally acceptable emergencies involving firemen, the police, or ambulance service.

Recognizing that independent living for older people is impossible without adequate income, health services, and decent housing, there is still an important role for the social support system, both formal and informal. Well and independent elderly, usually found among the younger, postretirement cohort aged 65 to 75, rely on informal social supports. This is supplemented to some extent by formal services in the area of socialization, senior center, nutrition sites, and assistance in using the recreational, educational, and cultural facilities of the community. Information on entitlements is also important to this age group, and children, friends, and neighbors are important channels through which such information flows. The emphasis among the well and comparatively well is still on independence and self motivation.

For persons moving into the stages of greater frailty, including those comparatively well, as well as those no longer self-sufficient to carry out the tasks of daily living, the services of the formal support structure loom more importantly. Particular needs include services in the home, counseling for themselves and their families on future alterations to independent living, transportation, and medical care. But even among these elderly, unless health fails completely, it is the informal system which bears the brunt of providing necessary assistance at times of crisis and in daily tasks of living. The informal socialization opportunities provided by kin and neighbors are also vital for such elderly.

Finally, as older people reach the age of greatest frailty, illness, and functional incapacity (usually around 85 or older), the balance will undoubtedly tip toward greater responsibility for their welfare being assumed by formal organizations. In this stage it is unlikely that many families, even with assistance, could supply the kinds of specialized services needed. Furthermore, the burden on younger family members would become too enormous and expensive.

Possibly the greatest problem in the field of aging is the paucity of empirical data. Here we can quickly point to just some of the important questions which need to be addressed.

Who is supporting or assisting older people to remain independent in the community? Are the support systems similar for different ethnic and socioeconomic groups? To what extent is the present system in accord with the preferences of older people? How do the systems provide the necessary support? What is the appropriate role for each part of the system? How can the members of the informal support network, not only family but friends and neighbors, be helped to more effectively provide assistance? What types of assistance, both monetary and programmatic, are needed from the government or the community for primary groups to continue in their roles as social support to older people? What is the nature of the interaction that occurs between the two systems, the formal or organizational and the primary group or informal system? And assuming that interaction occurs, what are the factors that will ensure that this interaction will really be psychologically and instrumentally successful? This is still unclear. It is not known whether there is a potential for partnership between the informal and the formal systems or whether there is only potential for conflict.

Then, it is necessary to go into the whole area of how we can actually tap the rich resources that are potentially available and determine what older people prefer in the informal support system. The issue of resources is particularly relevant today, given the increase in the number of elderly, the large numbers of frail elderly, and the changing roles of women. With more women entering the labor force the situation is changing because women are the major sources of support in the informal system. And then, finally, we have to address the issue of what is going to happen to tomorrow's elderly. Older people are going to be better educated, more affluent, and possibly more mobile. With respect to minorities such as the Hispanics, they will be more acculturated to the dominant white culture. The white culture has discarded the extended family value and now stresses independence and self-sufficiency. These values are often in conflict with the problems of older people as they become more dependent. What will be the support system in respect to this new generation of elderly? The issue of the operation of the informal support system and its relation to the formal system needs further research. Unless we know more about it, we really are in a very weak position with regard to social policy. And it will be difficult to enhance the life of old people.

POLITICAL
PERSPECTIVES

7

OLD-AGE POLITICS IN
A PERIOD OF CHANGE

Robert B. Hudson

The past decade has seen a great rekindling of interest in the politics of aging. The volume and variety of books, research monographs, and articles have risen dramatically. This growth, coupled with a new salience of the aging in politics, is now at a point where some students of the field are calling for full recognition of a new subfield under the rubric of "political gerontology" (Cutler, 1977; Estes, 1978).

A number of factors lie behind this expanded professional and lay interest. Perhaps most important is the recent massive expansion of public policy authorizations and expenditures made on behalf of the aging. Since 1965, public enactments providing exclusive or considerable benefits to the elderly include Medicare, Medicaid, the Older Americans Act, Supplemental Security Income, the Social Security Amendments of 1972 and 1977, Section 202 housing, and the Title XX legislation. At the state and local levels, "circuit breaker" and other property tax relief legislation, discount fares and special equipment in transportation, prescription drug rebates, low cost or free educational opportunities, and income tax relief all assist some or most older persons. The costs of the federal programs —including the massive Old Age and Survivors Insurance Program—are now in excess of $100 billion annually. And, much as "function follows financing," so too does research. Funds earmarked for research and demonstration accompany most of the federal program authorizations.

Also contributing to the increase of interest and research is the new prominence of the aging in the policy process — both as participants and beneficiaries of the policies. Again, much of this phenomenon can be attributed to policies themselves; policy is an important independent variable structuring politics, both generating and channeling political interest. Political activity has always been high among older persons, and the increased public sector involvement in affairs of the aging has created specific policy areas where the aging have a stake. The volume and level of older persons' participation in politics has generated research interest in how the elderly participate in politics and what may be the consequence. Research into the effects of age per se on political participation and inclinations has jumped several-fold in quantity and sophistication.

Similarly, interest and concern with the role of the organized aging in the policy process has been reflected in research. Beginning in the early 1960s, the mass-based old age organizations and aging-oriented professional and provider groups have been heavily engaged in working for the expansion of old age policies and toward cementing the allegiance of their memberships. The orientations and effectiveness of these organizations have been of increasing interest to members of the research community, particularly those in political science and sociology. As the aging of the population has widening social and political ramifications, this interest cannot but escalate. Finally, the professional research community, ever-mindful of its own imperatives, has seized on the interest in, and importance of, older persons to create and prosper from a new area of professional endeavor. Often working under the aegis of professional associations identified with gerontology, researchers in the politics of aging have increased both their numbers and output.

The major purpose here is to assess the yield of this increased level of research activity. A particular bias here is in the direction of accounting for the current state of old age policy, emphasizing the major factors responsible for its development to this point and the components of need that it addresses. While it is both necessary and proper to treat an array of questions related to politics and aging, the emphasis here is on politics relevant to public policy. It seeks to provide greater parity between the applied and knowledge-building functions of social research and is done primarily to overcome the "much ado about nothing" phenomenon found in much social research including, but obviously not confined to, the politics of aging.

Each of the sections below begins with a general discussion of the major findings and conclusions of past research, and this is followed by a discussion of the areas in need of new or additional exploration. Of central concern in these latter discussions are the issues concerning the relative and absolute growth which will occur in the older population in the decades ahead. More precisely, it will be argued that we are presently beginning to experience a change in longstanding patterns regarding the place of older persons in the policy process. In the past two years alone, more interest and concern have been voiced about public policy and aging than at any time since the enactment of the original Social Security legislation and the passage of Medicare. And this time, the interest developed will not quietly recede to the background. Growing numbers of older persons, enormous increases in the volume and level of

benefits, inflation and slow-growth economies are all com-
bining to place aging policy on the front burner and keep it
there.

The first section reviews research findings addressing patterns of older persons' political participation, the political
cohesion of older persons as political participants, and variations produced when investigation is confined to age-salient
issues. The second section deals with aging-based and aging-
oriented interest groups and discusses the ways in which old
age policy interests are filtered through these groups. The third
section looks to the relative scope and adequacy of policies
affecting the aging, emphasizing that a great deal has been
done but that unmet and growing problems still leave much
in need of attention. The fourth section suggests what factors
have aided the elderly in attaining their relatively favorable
policy standing and how the political base that has helped
yield past benefits may be shifting in fundamental ways.

THE AGING IN POLITICS

OVERVIEW OF CURRENT KNOWLEDGE

Current research related to the levels of interest and participation in the political process suggests older persons to be a
relatively active population grouping but provides little evidence suggesting that increasing age alters political inclinations assumed earlier in life. But, where attention is devoted
to specific issues that can differentially be viewed by persons
of different ages, variations in positioning by age cohort are
to be found. Shifts in the orientations of the population generally over time are more the results of socialization of new entry
cohorts into the population rather than significant reorienta-
tions of older cohorts. The limited evidence available reveals
that older cohorts are not immutable to shift in orientations,
but these tend to be somewhat more delayed and less marked

on specific political issues, however, variations are found in responses among different age cohorts. Thus, age—or, more precisely, time of birth—is of increasing political relevance as the inquiry moves from the general to the specific. Because age is the principal criterion in establishing eligibility for many policy benefits (education for the young, Social Security for the old) and because the expenditures for policies assisting the old are growing rapidly, the import of age in conditioning issue attitudes can be expected to grow as well.

The high levels of political interest and participation among older persons have been demonstrated conclusively. Numerous studies have shown it to increase steadily with age, peaking in the latter middle years, and falling off gradually in old age (Tingston, 1937; Lipset, 1960). When controls for level of education and for sex are introduced, however, the decline among the old is other than age-based (Glenn and Grimes, 1968; Verba and Nie, 1972). Only in the more active forms of participation beyond voting does age bring a diminution of involvement (Verba and Nie, 1972; Nie, Verba and Kim, 1974). Glenn (1969) finds no decline in interest in national or international affairs among the elderly, and his analysis of 35 cross-sectional and longitudinal surveys indicates greater interest among the elderly in current public figures than among younger persons with similar educational backgrounds.

Contemporary data addressing the fundamental political orientation of conservatism and liberalism suggest that individuals who are old may be somewhat more conservative than the remainder of the adult population, but the preponderance of the data does not support the contention that persons become increasingly conservative with age (Cutler, 1977). Glenn (1974) finds that persons beyond middle age have become more liberal, but that this increase in liberalism has not kept pace with changes in a liberal direction among the larger adult population. Thus, in *relative* terms, older persons are somewhat more conservative, but in *absolute* terms they have become more liberal. Voting studies employing party identification as a measure of the stability of orientations (this stressing the temporal rather than the substantive meaning of conservatism) show older persons demonstrating more stability, but various controls suggest this stability to be more a function of duration than age (Campbell et al., 1960; Butler and Stokes, 1971). As to earlier studies suggesting that aging brings with it an increase in Republican voting (Republicanism employed as a surrogate variable for conservatism), subsequent investigations suggest that older persons' Republican voting is based more on cohort than aging effects (Cutler, 1969; Glenn and Hefner, 1972). Searing et al. (1976), Glenn and Hefner (1972) and Jennings and Niemi (1975) have also noted the influence of period or historical effects in the determination and shifts in political orientations over time. Definitive sorting out of life cycle, cohort, and historical effects proves to be a virtually impossible task of disentangling age and time. The methodological limitations of the studies done to date are succinctly captured by Glenn (1974): "Whereas cross-sectional data confound aging effects with cohort effects, longitudinal data confound aging effects with period effects."

Where specific issues rather than general orientations are at question, existing evidence suggests greater age-based variations. On selected "group benefit" questions (Campbell et al., 1960), variations are found and seem readily interpretable by *cui bono* criteria. Even here, however, the variations in responses between different age groups tend not to be great. The issue area where age differences are the greatest and most consistent is health. Campbell et al. (1960) found older persons clearly more in favor of governmental involvement in health care financing, and analysis of more recent data from the University of Michigan Presidential election surveys revealed a similar distribution (Bengtson & Cutler, 1976). Schreiber and Marsden (1972) found in four surveys taken around the time of

Presidential elections from 1956 to 1968 that the aged consistently were more in favor of a governmental medical aid program than were younger persons. Weaver (1976) also noted the favorable positioning of the aged on the health issue and discusses it in terms of the aging as a "political community." There is limited and scattered evidence that where policy beneficiaries have clearly not been the aged; namely, in public education, older persons are more opposed to increased expenditures (Campbell, 1971; Clemente, 1975). In many areas, however, the aged and others are secondary beneficiaries and thus support may be forthcoming. As stated by Foner:

> Membership in an age-heterogeneous economic unit such as the family enables people of one age to benefit indirectly from programs directed at people of other ages. Specifically, pensions and Medicare relieve younger family members of the burden of caring for the old; or aid for the college education of the young eases the financial obligation of their middle-aged parents. In the shop, young people may be motivated to support liberal pensions for older workers as opening up jobs for themselves by easing older workers out of them [1972].

While it remains important to establish the extent to which the variations in political orientations and attitudes are attributable by age, the most prominent finding of the preponderance of these studies is that age-related factors alone account for relatively small amounts of variation among respondents. Economic status, education, ethnicity, and sex continue to be stronger determinants of attitudes than does age on all but the most central age-relevant issues. The bulk of the available survey data deals with national issues and orientations, and it may be that the concentration of older persons in certain states and localities and the greater specificity of many issues at those levels make for subnational variations in this generalization. Evidence to that effect is yet to be systematically gathered. House Speaker Thomas P. O'Neill, for example, has asserted that senior citizens in the state, who he said have been "hurt by

the administration," played a key role in the defeat of Gover-
nor Michael Dukakis in the 1978 Massachusetts primary elections. O'Neill knows a good deal more about Massachusetts
politics than most political scientists, but his assertion and
others like it need substantiation.

RESEARCH NEEDS

The often asserted potential of more cohesive participation
of the aged in state and local politics is a first major question
needing more explicit attention. The notion is not only intui-
tively appealing, but, as has been argued by Douglass et al.
(1974), issues of direct and immediate relevance to persons
yield greater variations over both time and issue than found
with attitudes and behaviors that are more fundamental and
which are anchored by early socialization. Where local issues,
such as school expansion or closings, property tax increase
or relief, and zoning issues are seen as both salient and subject
to remedy through political participation, variations by age
and other variables may be expected. Implicit here and also in
need of investigation is the sense of efficacy older voters
(Bengtson and Cutler, 1974) and others have in state and local
politics. Much folklore and some wisdom suggests that subnational governments are more responsive to popular pressures than is the federal government, but, as McConnell (1967)
and Fesler (1965) have forcefully argued, democracy need not
flourish in small jurisdictions. In a period of more restricted
governmental spending, questions of salience and efficacy will
assume new import for the aging and other groups that have
been beneficiaries of state and local governmental expenditures.

This leads to a second area very much in need of investigation, focusing on what—in the language of sociopolitical
gerontology—may be "the period effect" of our time. Known
commonly as the "Proposition 13" phenomenon, the current

popular concern with lower taxes, less spending, and "less government in our lives" has been building since the early 1970s. There is no reason to think that these concerns will not grow and become more intense well into the 1980s. While it is difficult and risky to label periods while they are in process, there can be no question that the concern with government and its costs is the most pervasive political concern of the present decade.

That this trend might have rather direct effects on aging politics and policy is not difficult to argue, and research in this area is clearly warranted. First, we need to know if the widespread topical concern with governmental growth and spending is being transmitted to present younger generations with sufficient intensity and consistency to be considered an emergent element relevant to political socialization. If these concerns prove to be short-lived and spasmodic, are shown to be limited to certain types of governmental activity, if they lessen with the easing of inflation, or are largely confined to populations already known to be disproportionately conservative, then the question of intergenerational transmission of these intense but only short-lived concerns can be dismissed. But, the possibility of such restrictive sentiments about governmental activity being more than transitory should not be dismissed.

Toward the other end of the age spectrum, we also need greater information about the ways in which contemporary attitudes toward public policy are being received and generated by other persons. The question of intensity and duration arises here as well. More specifically, this raises an issue that has received only passing attention to the point; namely, understanding older persons as taxpayers. As material alluded to earlier would make clear, there are most certainly great variations among older persons on tax matters, but the present environment calls for closer investigation of tax questions. Scattered evidence shows that older people have tended to resist increased governmental activity where—unlike medical care—they are not prime beneficiaries (Killian and Haer, 1958; Hunt, 1960; Campbell, 1971). There is also scattered evidence that older persons have disproportionately favored recent referenda initiatives to limit state and local public spending.

It is important—both for the larger public and the aging themselves—to know the extent to which the aging population will be lending its growing numbers to the movement toward lessened governmental activity. The question is particularly intriguing because the elderly—at least at the national level—currently receive public benefits far out of proportion to their numbers. It is more than understandable that significant numbers of older persons, as with the general population, are threatened and bothered by current levels of taxation. The older population may contribute, however, to a backlash should it be found or perceived that they are moving in large numbers to cut overall spending while continuing to demand that their own relatively privileged tax position be maintained. A potential, second-order consequence may be that divisions among the aging population concerning taxes and spending will create new policy schisms within the ranks of the elderly. Most would identify with the recently convened Ad Hoc Coalition of National Organizations on Aging, designed to protect spending programs, but increasing pressures on the tax side—advocated and subscribed to by some older persons—could produce discord as well as coalescence.

THE ORGANIZED AGING

OVERVIEW OF CURRENT KNOWLEDGE

Among the most notable developments in American politics in the last quarter century has been the massive increase of organized groups pressing claims in the public sector. In con-

junction with the continuing decline in the role of political
parties in structuring the political universe, this development
has produced a fragmented political pattern that Theodore
Lowi (1969) labelled "interest group liberalism" and what
Newsweek has dubbed more recently the era of "single issue
politics."

The emergence of a contemporary politics of aging illu-
strates this pattern. After an early history marked by occasional episodes of concerted social action—the Townsend
Movement of the 1930s (Holtzman, 1963) and the McLain
Movement in California in the 1950s (Pinner et al., 1959)—
organized aging groups fell largely from the scene. Since the
early 1960s, however, new groups have sprung to life and have
developed bureaucratic structures and routinized patterns of
action that clearly set them apart from those groups or move
ments which had gone before (Pratt, 1976). As do most other
groups pressing their demands in Washington, these groups
concern themselves with limited and incremental change and
very much reflect the pattern of interest group liberalism
(Binstock, 1972). In addition to these mass-based organizations (claiming memberships totalling more than fifteen million older persons), organizations of advocates, providers,
researchers, and public agencies have emerged. There is no
question that, in the words of Dale Vinyard (1978), "the aging
have been rediscovered."

The volume of literature devoted to contemporary old age
interest groups continues to be limited. It consists of works by
Pratt (1974, 1976), Binstock (1972), and Vinyard (1978).
Pratt's study, *The Gray Lobby* (1976) offers a detailed picture
of the development and overall orientation of the major aging-
based interest groups: the American Association of Retired
Persons (AARP), the National Council of Senior Citizens
(NCSC), and the National Association of Retired Federal
Employees (NARFE); and the principal aging-oriented
groups: the Gerontological Society, the National Council on

the Aging (NCOA), and the National Association of State Units on Aging (NASUA). Particularly regarding the mass-based groups, he provides a lengthy and informed narrative of their growth and their activity in selective policy areas. Apart from its importance as an historical account, Pratt's book highlights aspects of the aging organizations' growth and development that have affected both the direction and effectiveness of their policy related activities.

Several policy-relevant themes are sounded in the writings on aging interest groups. First, internecine disputes have diminished their collective impact on the policy process. The American Association of Retired Persons did not join other groups in supporting the Medicare legislation, and AARP and NCSC have differed over the merits of liberalizing mandatory retirement legislation. The aging groups also contended with each other in trying to gain access to an indirect control over different social service and manpower programs designed to assist the elderly (Binstock, 1972). In other areas and at other times, however, the aging organizations have presented more of a common front. Coalescence has occurred around broad issues where much of the aging population is affected (favoring Social Security increases; decrying coinsurance increases under Medicare), where recognition of aging as an area of public concern can be promoted (White House Conferences on Aging, the status of Administration of Aging within HEW; the creation of a National Institute on Aging within NIH, creation of special committees), and where the collective well-being of the aging enterprise is under threat (the early Nixon years and in the present period of threatened austerity). With funding levels having increased for most aging programs in the mid-1970s and with many programs having become more institutionalized, there has also been a lessening of tension and skirmishing.

How present pressures will affect these more settled relations is still an open question. The creation of the Ad Hoc Coalition, suggests that the groups may hang together rather than hang separately, but these new pressures must nonetheless be expected to have unsettling consequences for aging interests, both public and private. Thus, the current leadership of the Administration on Aging is promoting a more concentrated effort in long-term care. Its doing so is, at least in part, a response to growing outside concern about what purposes the Older Americans Act appropriations are serving. This emphasis, however, may cause disruptions in the relations between the state and area agencies and the providers of those services that may be given lower priority in the future. Further disruptions may occur should a strategy of creating substate, long term care authorities be adopted. The state agencies would have an uncertain role under such a system, and the area or other agencies given this new mandate would be in more of a regulatory than a disbursement role. In sum, should moves of this kind develop, the recognition and servicing role that allows internal differences to be minimized might be replaced by a more instrumental and functional role in which heads would be knocked and tensions would be inevitable.

The activities and orientations of aging-oriented organizations are shaped in part by their membership bases and professional associations. The National Council of Senior Citizen's membership base comes from organized labor; NCOA's membership is almost entirely from the social welfare community; the Gerontological Society's is from the research community, planners, and practice professionals. The ties between the largest of the groups, AARP, and the Colonial Penn Life Insurance Company, and the implications of those ties have recently been the subject of heated controversy (Mintz, 1979). The general concern with these kinds of memberships and affiliations is an important one, namely, the extent to which the groups are working on behalf of the aging—as they all claim— as contrasted with their using the aging to pursue organizational ends of their own. The AARP/Colonial Penn linkage

has received the most attention, but the Gerontological Society
has been castigated on several recent occasions by the Gray
Panthers on grounds which, at least conceptually, are rather
similar (Kuhn/Maddox exchange, 1978). The particular ways
these well-known dysfunctions are introduced by organized
concerns in the aging field have been discussed in Estes (1974),
Hudson (1974), and Binstock and Levin (1976). The tensions
created by organizational imperatives can also be expected to
increase as aging dollars become tighter and demands for service results become more intense.

The responsiveness of aging-oriented groups to the aging
and their needs is also affected by the organizations' internal
structures. Borrowing from McCarthy and Zald, Vinyard
(1978) observes that (a) large portions of the organizations'
resources come from outside the aggrieved group; (b) the
effective membership bases are much smaller than what is
officially claimed; (c) the leadership cadres are more often professionals than constituents; and (d) claims that each of the
groups speaks for the entire aging constituency are misleading.
As Binstock has argued, the belief in policy circles that one or
more of these groups do, in fact, speak for "the aging" may
create the illusion of power and representativeness and thus
be functional for some numbers of older persons as well as the
groups themselves. But the mix of interests being represented,
however effectively, remains in question. Positive results can
emerge from the latitude afforded organizational leaders and
their staffs. Thus, the difference of the aging groups has provided behind-the-scenes support to the work of the National
Senior Citizens Law Center in some of its litigation regarding,
for example, administrative rulings under the SSI program. It
can be presumed that many members of these groups would
not endorse the use of their resources to pursue public interest
law and welfare objectives.

Both Pratt and Binstock present useful material on the
nature of the relations which develop between the professional

staffs of these groups and public officials. As has been observed
in a number of policy areas—business (Bauer et al.,
1963), education (Murphy, 1971), and medical care (Feder, 1977)—
group success is not so much about pressure as it is about the
exchange of information and support. The present aging interest groups are well-suited to the development and maintenance of these kinds of relations. As Pratt suggests, it would
be extremely difficult for nonbureaucratized and structured
mass movements of the kind associated with Townsend and
McLain to engage in this kind of activity. The mutual interests
of private and public actors operating in the same policy area —
such as aging—constitute a key element of the phenomenon of
interest group liberalism or what Roger Davidson (1977) refers
to as "cozy triangles" and Robert Salisbury (1968) as "self-
regulation." They have developed readily in the aging world
because of the overall "benign environment" (Pratt) in which
aging has found itself until recently.

NEEDED RESEARCH

Three interrelated areas -none of which is unexplored—
need further research. The first involves a more thorough understanding of the policy relevant positions taken by the private and public aging organizations and more refined knowledge of the priority given, and energy invested in, different of
their purported interests. Different works cited earlier present
relatively brief summary statements of the private organizations' positions on major issues, but, in addition to their brev-
ity, they present little evidence for the relative weighting the
organizations give to different policy issues and alternatives.

Of particular interest in this regard is the stand taken and
resources committed to policies affecting the disadvantaged
elderly. It is now widely held in the extant literature that these
organizations pursue incremental rather than fundamental

162 AGING AND SOCIETY

options. The reasoning behind this choice is familiar to students of organizations and interest groups: Leadership sets the organizational agenda largely on its own; uses its mailings and meetings to convince membership of the leadership's choices; engages public officials using the implicit message that—as Binstock has put it—"our X number of members stand united behind Option Y"; sees some level of their recommendations into law; and returns to the membership telling it of their organization's success. As this argument goes, the agenda items selected must be incremental. This set of two-way communications with members and officials must produce some policy results to convince members of the organization's efficacy. The original options chosen, so the argument goes, must be largely on the margins and thus more readily adaptable as law. This may, in fact, accurately describe the operations and reasoning of the aging interest groups, but the actual evidence marshalled to this effect remains rather skimpy.

More fundamental than this question of interest group choice is what Edelman (1960) has called the quiescent function served by organized groups. While we do not know as much as we should concerning the meaningful priorities of the different groups, it is clear, from any reading of their literature, that they speak to a very broad array of aging-related issues. In so doing, these groups work to cement organizational loyalties and, less directly, to preclude the development of potentially rival movements. Thus, while a literal reading of the organizations' literature and proclamations suggests an almost endless attempt to rally members into action, its real effect—partially intended—is pacification. The message is "yes, you do have a number of problems, but don't worry, we're working on them." Actual solutions may or may not follow; what is important is the appearance that something is being done. What are no more than symbols take on a reality of their own, and, as put by Harold Lasswell, "political symbolization has its cathartic function" (Lasswell, 1930). It seems certain that aging interest groups, knowingly or not, perform this function. In conjunction with the personal and social disabilities suffered by the most disadvantaged elderly, it strongly suggests that "the scope and bias of the pressure system" (Schattschneider, 1960) not only does not greatly aid the disadvantaged elderly but works to preclude efforts by them and others to remedy their situation.

Engaging in research concerning what does not happen is a longstanding problem in the social sciences. It is no easier in the aging field than elsewhere, but the case of the Gray Panthers is of considerable interest in this context. The Panthers were "convened" several years ago by Maggie Kuhn and see themselves working toward a cross-generational alliance aimed at creating a meaningful and nonstereotypical place for older persons in society. Their members have castigated the research community for treating older persons as "objects" and have attacked all of the organized aging groups for using the elderly simply to promote their own professional and organizational concerns. They oppose the emphasis on services (and "servers"), such as the nutrition program, because older persons are presented with products rather than being involved as individuals. The question in the present context is whether the Gray Panthers can expand their very limited ranks with their current credo intact, whether they must adopt (or fall into) the institutionalizing patterns—and quiescent functions—associated with organizational maturation, or whether they will slowly fade from the scene. There are any number of reasons for suggesting that they will meet with the second or third alternative, but the Gray Panthers are the only contemporary entity that comes anywhere close—despite their small numbers—to resembling the movements associated with aging in earlier years.

A final question addresses the issue of power. A professional debate has gone on for some years now over whether these groups are powerful or influential, whether they may only appear to be but, in fact, are not, and whether this distinction makes any difference. The question will be addressed in the broader context of factors associated with aging policies in this chapter's concluding section, but one observation is in order here. These questions concerning power have not been effectively answered in part because of other circumstances surrounding the aging policy sphere. But changes in this environment are now underway making it considerably less "benign" (Pratt). What this changing situation may produce, among other things, is a more definitive test of how much power—involving rewards and sanctions—the elderly and their groups really have. This is an important question; and new realities may provide a laboratory where it can be investigated and the consequences measured.

THE CURRENT STATUS OF OLD AGE POLICY

Three overarching statements neatly, if only generally, capture the essence of contemporary public policies toward the aging: (a) The level of governmental "effort" on behalf of older persons, as measured by almost any index, has risen dramatically over the last two decades; (b) This effort has contributed significantly to the improved income status among the overall aging population; and (c) There continues to be considerable unmet need among longstanding and often growing subpopulations of the elderly. Our information is relatively comprehensive about what has been done for the elderly in general, reasonably adequate concerning what remains to be done, but remains only fragmentary as regards how what are known to be needed improvements can be brought about. To the last item, there are two discrete pieces: a political and economic question asking how needed resources can be generated and an implementation question asking what intervention alternatives and strategies should be employed within existing and projected fiscal constraints.

The increase in governmental authorizations and publicly mandated old age expenditures have been among the least noticed but most dramatic policy developments of the contemporary period. Only during the past year has the magnitude of this growth come to center stage (Samuelson, 1978; Califano, 1978; Hudson, 1978; National Journal, 1978). The concern and controversy surrounding these reports, the marked trend they highlight, and the implications that flow from them are easily understandable. Of the 47 major programs included in the House Select Committee on Aging's booklet, "Federal Responsibility to the Elderly" (1977), three-quarters have been enacted since 1960. An earlier and different count from the same committee placed the number of programs assisting the elderly at 134, with a somewhat higher percentage of these having been added during the same period. While many of these programs involve only modest expenditures, the volume of legislative activity represented in these numbers belie the notion that older persons have been somehow neglected, either during the "youth" decade of the 1960s or the "retrenchment" decade of the 1970s.

The more concrete indicator of aging policy growth, however, lies in the rapid rise in federal expenditures for older persons. Spending under the Old Age and Survivors Insurance (OASI) portion of Social Security has tripled between 1970 and 1979. Medicare expenditures for the elderly have increased nearly ten times since the program's inception in 1965. Federal grants to the states for the elderly under Medicaid care are now at $3.5 billion, and now 40% of Medicaid expenditures assist the elderly (principally for nursing home care). Health care expenditures for older persons under the Veterans Administration—America's closest approximation to socialized medicine (Sapolsky, 1977)—are currently estimated at $2.5 billion (Iglehart, 1978). Retirement and insurance benefits for federal civilian and military employees now stand at roughly $20 billion, a four-fold increase since 1969. When these major programs are combined with the large number of social service, housing, transportation, research, and training programs, current expenditures targeted for the elderly total over $130 billion (U.S. Office of Management and Budget, 1979).

Turning to the second general observation, there is no doubt that the overall aging population is considerably better off than it was ten or twenty years ago. Part of this improvement lies in factors other than direct governmental expenditures for older persons. Successive cohorts of older persons are better educated, enjoyed better health care during their early and middle years, and some are now better able to provide for their retirement years because of maturing private pension schemes. It is clear, however, that government sponsored and financed programs have also had a positive effect, although it is difficult to know precisely how much.

A variety of standard indicators show the improvements in well-being, if not the causes. Life expectancy for persons aged 40 has increased by nearly three years since 1940 (U.S. Bureau of the Census, 1975). Health among the elderly—as measured by numbers of "restricted activity days"—has improved markedly since the mid-1950s. There has been a leveling off in this trend among the 65+ population during the 1970s (National Center for Health Statistics, 1969, 1974, 1978), but this is likely due to the growing number of persons 75+ in the aging population. It should also be noted that other indices of functional disability have shown less marked improvement (Shanas, 1978). It is in income that the most dramatic overall improvements have been made. Poverty among the elderly, as measured by the Census Bureau (1977), has shown a marked decline: from 35% of the older population in 1959 to 14% in 1977 A considerably larger number of older persons remain in the "near poor" category (125% of the poverty measure), but other estimates put the percentage of older persons in poverty even lower than the Census Bureau estimate. University of Wisconsin poverty researchers see just over 5% of older persons in poverty (Watts and Skidmore, 1977), and the Congressional Budget Office (1977)—factoring in in-kind programs such as Medicare, food stamps, and housing benefits—places the figure at just above 4%. The CBO report is of particular significance in that it contends that 58% of older persons would be in poverty in the absence of governmental programs. Of the programs that have contributed to this improvement, most notable is OASI where average monthly benefits have increased six-fold since 1950 and have more than doubled since the mid-1960s.

Despite these growing expenditures and data showing an improvement in the well-being of the overall aging population, severe and widespread problems continue to exist among major aging subpopulations. The median income of a single older person is only $3,495 compared to $8,721 for older couples and $7,030 for single persons under age 65. The median income of the black elderly is $2,739 as contrasted with $5,644 for older whites. Nowhere are the differences between younger and older populations and younger-old and old-old more pronounced than in health status. Morbidity, mortality, and a variety of functional disabilities all increase with age. For those suffering from economic hardship and loneliness as well, old age often brings with it double and triple jeopardy.

Public policies have brought some relief. Social Security's progressive benefit formula provides much higher replacement rates for low income contributors (and also, it should be added, for higher income, short-term contributors); SSI provides an inadequate but guaranteed income to the poorest old and disabled; Medicare now provides relatively low cost acute care coverage to virtually the entire older population; Medicaid provides acute and long-term care coverage to the poorest of the aged; means-tested housing, food stamps, and social service programs target increasing, though still inadequate, resources on the low income older population.

There are several reasons—some inherent in program design and others associated with program implementation—why the massive public expenditures targeted for the older population leave substantial numbers of older persons disadvantaged. First, while liberalization of benefits in the income programs has been dramatic in recent years, the base-rate on which improvements have been made was sufficiently low that current benefits for many remain inadequate. Thus, while OASI benefits have increased six-fold since 1950, the average benefit in 1950 on which that increase is based was only $64. Low-income workers also receive benefits, which alone are inadequate to live on. Even though the benefit formula is weighted toward such persons through a disproportionately high rate of replacement on working years income (Schulz, 1976), the base rate is often sufficiently low to preclude an adequate income through Social Security benefits alone. The system historically was not intended to provide by itself adequate retirement income and is, in fact, built around concern with both equity (return related to contributions: a social insurance function) and adequacy (return related to need: a social welfare function). Thus, despite this latter element of Social Security, higher benefits go to persons with higher working years income and the contributions based on those incomes.

Whether one could or would like to reallocate a greater portion of OASI benefits toward the lowest income groups, given the historical and popular assumptions behind the program's purpose and the separate contributions made into it, is open to question. Analysts such as Alicia Munnell (1976) have argued that any changes made should be in the opposite direction, namely, placing benefits more in line with past contributions. Moves of this kind, in fact, received official sanction in the Carter Administration's fiscal year 1980 budget: The relative advantages afforded low-income workers through the benefit structure would be reduced by eliminating the minimum $122 monthly benefit. This proposal is designed to reduce the windfall benefits which accrue to higher income persons who have contributed for a minimum period, but it will also place some low-income, long-time contributors under the SSI program.

Targeting of resources is an issue in other policy areas affecting the older population. While the elderly on an aggregate and per capita basis receive far higher public dollar support than does the younger population, nearly 80% of government financed personal health care benefits was spent for older persons defined as nonpoor compared to 51% spent for nonpoor persons in the remainder of the population. Ever-increasing out-of-pocket health expenditures (higher even than before Medicare) and increasing "co-insurance" payments under Medicare also place a particularly heavy burden on the disadvantaged elderly. Distribution questions also arise regarding the treatment of older persons in the tax code. There is no question that older persons generally are favorably treated by exemption of Social Security and Railroad Retirement benefits, double personal exemption, a retirement income credit, and the recent $100,000 exemption from capital gains tax of the sale of a principal residence for persons aged 55 and above. While all persons above the stipulated age are eligible for these deductions and exemptions, they, in fact, provide disproportionate benefits to those older persons with higher incomes.

In sum, nearly one-quarter of the federal budget is targeted for older persons; and, in part because of the effort reflected in this enormous expenditure, large numbers of older persons are better off than before. But an equally persistent reality—due in part to the distribution of these funds and in part to the range and intensity of need of the disadvantaged elderly—is that one-seventh of the elderly remain in poverty and an equal number consider themselves in poor health. The increasing numbers of older persons—and especially the very old—in the years ahead, declining rates of mortality among the older population, and expected difficulties (due to both economic and demographic factors) in paying for needed benefits are issues in need of debate and research.

RESEARCH NEEDS

The debate about the future of public policy for the aging must revolve around a triad of concerns: need, equity, and cost. Ideally, one would meet all legitimate need on an equitable basis, within cost parameters that would not be onerous to direct contributors or taxpayers generally, and which would not infringe on other legitimate areas of domestic public spending. The values underpinning this set, however, are sufficiently divergent, and the actual context in which they must be played out is sufficiently constrained that trade-offs are necessary and inevitable.

In this critical debate now emerging, the research community should first see to it that alternative policy proposals and intervention strategies emerge that incorporate concern with need as well as cost and, second, that the debate about the future course of public policy and aging—whatever course it takes—be informed regarding the consequences of alternative courses of action proposed. On the first point, events in 1978 were an important first step. The cost question had to be raised and was (Samuelson, 1978a). But by the end of the year the debate had broadened with concern for the vulnerable elderly in a period of austerity being a salient feature (Iglehart, 1978; Zander, 1978; Binstock, 1978). On the second point, research effort in long term care and income maintenance will be critical. Action in these areas is clearly in the offing, and research must inform the decisions made with regard to both possible options and likely consequences.

In long term care, critical actors in Washington, recognizing both current levels and future volume of need among the aging population, are beginning explorations on a number of fronts. In 1978, officials in HEW requested authority from the Office of Management and Budget to fund over $100 million for research and demonstrations into restructuring the long-term care delivery system. Because of the anti-inflation concerns of the administration, only a sum far lower than this ($30 million) has been approved, but the initiative's being pursued nevertheless speaks to the growing concern about the need for more appropriate and effective services for the chronically ill elderly. The Administration on Aging (AoA) has also made clear its intentions to make long-term care its priority in coming years. Regional centers for the study and demonstration of long-term care alternatives are the focal point of AoA's research, demonstration, and evaluation strategy for fiscal year 1979 and beyond. Potentially much more important is the likelihood that AoA will increasingly try to use its auspices— principally its state and local grantees funded through Title III of the Older Americans Act—to involve the aging "network" more centrally in the administration and delivery of long-term care services. These agencies have in recent years concentrated much of their effort in social services related to long term care, but the long term care mission has never been so explicitly explored. A less focused but longstanding role of the state and area agencies—serving as advocates for the entire aging population—seems almost certain to be downplayed if this more recent move develops in accordance with the intentions of AoA's new leadership.

A number of different mechanisms are being investigated on at least a preliminary basis by government and private researchers. One option calls for the use of new or existing agencies as the locus for the development of community-based long term care systems. The agencies operating such a system would perform traditional case management or triage functions but might also be called on to bring different of the existing long-term care funding streams—Medicare, Medicaid, Title XX, Title III—under a coordinating or more controlling authority. Area agencies on aging are being proposed as one vehicle through which this melding might be attempted. A second alternative would involve collapsing existing programs and appropriations into a bloc grant to the states for long-term care purposes with the states being relatively free to organize the delivery structure as they see fit. A third alternative, not necessarily incompatible with either of the first two, would involve the development of health maintenance organizations (HMOs) for the elderly. As with existing HMOs, these organizations would enroll older persons on a prepaid, capitated basis and would be legally obligated to provide them with needed services with no additional charges entailed. As with the earlier alternatives, many of the provisions under existing legislation would either have to be altered or waived. Insurance options have also been proposed, but these would involve major restructuring of the current system, and their development does not seem likely given current trends and exigencies.

In incomes, debate continues regarding questions of benefit adequacy, problems of future funding, and the role of public pensions as a source of retirement income. The massive Social Security tax package enacted in 1977, concern about the effect of that package on individual workers and the general economy, and the ever-present demographic trends have lent a renewed sense of urgency to these discussions. The adequacy question must remain paramount. On an aggregate basis, the picture for older persons is much improved, and the overall income position of the elderly vis-à-vis the younger population has also shown modest improvement. Yet, official measures continue to speak of minimum rather than adequate standards, and in terms of adequacy much remains to be done. The growing concern among moderate and upper income groups that they will get a poor return on their Social Security investment —as reflected in the new OASI "weighting" proposals—presents yet another potential impediment to addressing meaningfully the adequacy question. It is understandable why the better-off groups wonder about the wisdom of their forced investment; it is also clear that increasing numbers of this group will be able to add private pension benefits to whatever it is that Social Security provides.

Whatever strategies the analysts divine cannot but involve difficult choices. The most current proposals would place additional numbers of low income older persons under the Supplemental Security Income program which, despite its carefully chosen title, still smacks of "welfare" to many. It clearly involves means-testing, which advocates and others find a throwback to an earlier era. The program has also had problems in implementation during its early years (Zander, 1978). Citizen concern will continue to surround the Social Security system on both the benefit and cost sides. The 1977 tax increase understandably aroused the resentment of workers, but it has not relieved the anxieties of current and near-term beneficiaries who continue to worry about the system's fiscal integrity. In addition to that ongoing concern, the principal issue now emerging will be the extent to which the question of adequacy will be subordinated to maintenance of the Social Security's insurance function and to pressures from the constituency of current workers and moderate to well-off retirees who will most surely push in that direction.

The period of rapid growth in new initiatives and liberalization of spending under longstanding legislation appears, at least temporarily, to be at an end. Public policy costs under existing statutory obligations will rise at such a pace—because of demography and inflation—that improvements in the policy status of older people will have to concentrate on more effective use of resources now being spent or anticipated. And current projections may have to be honed if general economic conditions should change for the worse. Current assumptions about patterns of distribution—especially those where entitlement is based solely on chronological age—may have to give way to concern about adequate income and functional need. Much of this debate will transcend the special purview of persons identified with research, but such persons must raise the fundamental questions and provide the information on which informed—if controversial—decisions can be reached.

OLD AGE POLICY AND
A CHANGING POLITICAL ENVIRONMENT

Rising public policy costs, emerging demographic trends, growing unrest about taxes and spending, and concern among the range of interests supported through governmental auspices are changing the aging political universe. Their consequences for old age policy cannot be precisely estimated, but it is possible to suggest how some of the longstanding political "ground rules" of old age policy may be altered by these factors.

What seems most certain is that aging policy will be conducted in a more charged atmosphere than has historically been the case. Concern with the rate of growth of old age policy expenditures is already mounting in Washington, and popular pressure against these heavy expenditures may also increase as, in fact, it has already toward the Social Security system. From both a research and a policy perspective, this changing environment calls for greater attention to the factors which have supported the aging in politics and to models for understanding how they may continue to fare.

The model most conventionally used to explain policy outcomes—in the aging arena and elsewhere—treats popular demands and organized pressure as the central factors behind the enactment (or retention) of particular policy provisions or objectives. With some variations, political scientists in the 1950s and 1960s who subscribed to pluralist or group theories of the political process also sought to understand policy outcomes in demand/pressure terms. Certainly, both popular and professional concern with the make-up and behavior of political interest groups has as its principal assumption that the objectives and strengths of organized interests are the explanatory element behind public policy enactments.

Because the demand/pressure model has been so widely employed, its assumptions about the policy world should be set forth so that the model's utility and limitations can be explored. The demand/pressure model, narrowly construed, views the policy process as one in which:

(a) The most relevant occurrences or actions are those which take place among private groups and between private groups and governmental officials.

(b) A policy proposal which will aid one group will probably work to the detriment of another group. Most policies are "zero-sum," meaning that the benefits which accrue to one set of actors bring a roughly corresponding loss to some other set of actors.

(c) A group's successfully pursuing policy objectives is a function of its political power, viz., the ability to mobilize more resources (votes, dollars, information, technology, and the like) than can opposing groups.

(d) Most official decision makers are relatively neutral as to the substance of policy outcomes. Their decisions are based on their perception of the balance of forces around the question at hand, which, for them, translates into the balance of the inducements different groups can offer and the sanctions these groups can impose.

(e) Interest groups are indulged in the policy process in accordance with their actual or perceived power—the ability to offer inducements to and impose sanctions on governmental decision-makers.

Undoubtedly, much of politics and policy is about this model. But it does not incorporate all potentially relevant variables and its "dominant inference pattern"—pressure yielding policy—is not equally valid for all policy circumstances. Among the major factors which may condition or render largely inapplicable the demand/pressure model are the following:

(a) political culture: prevailing attitudes about the salience of certain issues, the legitimacy of different interests, and the appropriate role of government in addressing those issues and interests;

(b) perceptions and latitude of decision-making officials: the beliefs officials bring to the decision-making process as to what are actual needs and appropriate public responses and their own needs and resources which allow them to pressure and manipulate as well as be pressured and manipulated;

(c) types and functions of particular policies: the distribution of perceived benefits and costs as they relate to both the policy's manifest and latent purposes;

(d) governmental structure and policy channels: the locus and scope of decision-making bodies and the biases they introduce in the policy process;

(e) the ongoing policy context: the status and array of public policies which constitute the policy universe at any point in time and from which all new policy departures must be made.

Clearly, each of these factors shapes and conditions demands and pressures which may emerge, how such demands fare in the policy process, and how they may emerge as public policy, if at all. In fact, each of these elements or combinations of them may serve as alternate models to that stressing demands and pressures as means of understanding and accounting for policy outcomes. Elazar (1972) and Elazar and Zikmund (1975) have relied heavily on political culture in discussing the policy process in the American federal system, and Almond and Verba (1963), among many others, have used this concept in cross-national political studies. Theoretical and empirical works focusing on the role of decision-makers and other elites include Dahl (1967), Marvick (1961), Pressman and Wildavsky (1973), Derthick (1975), and many others. The content and functions of particular policies are featured in Edelman (1960), Lowi (1964), Redford (1969), and Wilson (1973). The import of governmental structure on policy-making in the United States —the federal system, separate governmental branches sharing functions, small and numerous political jurisdictions, fragmentation within the executive and congressional branches— has been employed as the central unit of analysis (McConnell, 1967; Fesler, 1965) and widely used elsewhere (Seidman, 1977;

Neustadt, 1960; Salisbury, 1968). Finally, the import of the cumulative and current policy landscape in shaping subsequent actions has been carefully treated by Lindblom (1959), Wildavsky (1964), and Heclo (1974). A very useful summary of models based on different of these factors is found in Dye (1972).

In the popular press and occasionally in works of a more scholarly nature, it is often assumed that the lobbying activities of older persons and their organizations have been the sole or paramount factor behind most old age policy enactments. In the publications of aging interest groups, the assumption is usually explicit. The shortcoming of arguments along this line—borrowing from the demand/pressure model—is not that they are "wrong" or necessarily inappropriate, but rather that they tend to concentrate on too narrow a range of relevant factors. The Townsend Movement was on officials' minds at the time of the original Social Security enactments, but, according to first-hand (Altmeyer, 1968) and retrospective (Schleslinger, 1958; Pratt, 1976) accounts, it did not play the decisive role attributed to it by Holtzman (1963). The National Council of Senior Citizens clearly served as an important publicist and exerted pressures, but its role was not so dominant as its claims would suggest (Marmor, 1970). The White House Conference on Aging in 1971 brought aging issues to the fore in early 1972, but was not so responsible for old age policy enactments in the subsequent two-year period as Pratt (1976) suggests (Hudson, 1978a).

To more fully understand the current state of aging policies (i.e., those *already* on the books), other factors must be brought to bear. The need in this regard is two-fold: first, because their use provides more adequate and informed understanding of past policy enactments, and, second, because it is changes in these very factors which may constitute a fundamental shift in the political bases of future old age politics.

How the five factors above relate to different old age enactments is not unknown, but their importance often goes un-
mentioned or unheeded. The American *political culture* has
been most critical to the aging policy process. No population
group in twentieth-century America has enjoyed more policy
legitimacy and engendered more concern than the elderly. Not
only were the elderly the principal beneficiaries of the revolutionary policies of the 1930s, but it was they who made possible
the massive entry of the federal government into the era of the
welfare state. Traditional American attitudes toward government activity not only prevented this type of activity but were
also central in precluding the institution of class-based politics
which might have fostered greater domestic governmental
involvement as it did in other industrial nations. This positive
attitude toward the needs of older persons was central 30 years
later with the passage of Medicare, and—as reflected in the
attitudes of Congress—was of crucial importance in the enactment of the Supplemental Security Income program. The
legitimacy older persons have enjoyed in American politics is
essential to any attempt to account for the benefits older
persons enjoy. It has not by itself been solely responsible—
no such distal factor could be—but the demonstrated willing-
ness of decision-makers and the populace alike to support
old age policy benefits undermines the "power of the aging"
arguments associated with the demand/pressure model.

The *interest of decision-makers* in affairs of the aging and
their latitude to act independently constitute a second kind of
political resource the elderly possess. Positive dispositions
toward the elderly result from a combination of concern with
the aging's plight and an interest in having expression of that
concern rebound to their own advantage. As an antidote to the
belief that elected politicians are little other than self-serving,
one need only look again to SSI. When the Senate Finance
Committee voted on the "adult minimum floor"—the essential
feature of what was to become SSI—former HEW Secretary

Wilbur Cohen announced jubilantly: "Do you realize what they're doing there! It's not even controversial! It's not even controversial! . . ." (Burke and Burke, 1974); but "they" do, in fact, provide a guaranteed income for three million older, blind, and disabled Americans. Presumably, Congress knew who it was helping, even if it did not know the nature of the breakthrough it was making or the precedent it might be setting.

But, more obviously political agendas are also at work when governmental incumbents indulge the aging. The Older Americans Act was little more than a statement of symbolic affirmation when it was enacted. That it has become a piece of major legislation—with appropriations currently in excess of $500 million—is more the result of continued symbolism, short-term political calculation, and normal accretion than it is of insistent demand by older persons' service needs. Other legislation that recognizes much more need than it meets—housing, transportation, senior employment—is cut from the same cloth. Certainly, there has been pressure for enactment and expansion of these policies, but the pressure of aging service providers and advocates cannot alone account for funding under a categorical social services program such as the Older Americans Act which has increased 156 times in 12 years. The additional factors here are what Mayhew (1974) refers to as advertising, credit claiming, and enacting "particularistic" benefits. Older persons and, more to the point, being on record as having assisted them are of great utility to elected officials. Again, pressure has helped, but is far from the only force at work.

The importance of the third general factor—*policy type and content*—follows closely from the above. The aging have done well in the policy arena in part because of who they are, but they have also done well along particular policy dimensions, that is, in terms of what kinds of benefits they have received. The preponderance of recent legislation enacted for the elderly has involved disbursing funds through state, local, or special governments to provide services or facilities for older persons. While the merit of these programs relative to alternative courses of public action may be debated, they are useful politically in that they are designed to assist a deserving population, are staffed by an infrastructure of professionals and providers, and spread the policy costs while concentrating the benefits. The regulatory aspect is usually confined only to purposes for which allocated funds may be spent. There have been exceptions (the recent mandatory retirement legislation being an important example) but distribution rather than regulation has been the hallmark of aging legislation of the last decade. Social Security is also something of an exception. Its magnitude is far greater, and, as an incomes program, its administrative infrastructure is proportionally much smaller than the in-kind service programs. Yet, until recently, it too has been a program where, as a matter of *perception*, benefits were concentrated and costs were widely distributed. As reported by Representative Abner Mikva, it was only with the 1977 tax increase that public sentiment shifted from massive support to great concern. And, as recently as 1972, Congressmen were falling over themselves to get on the bandwagon to increase OASDI benefits 20% across the board. This and other aging expenditures are not viewed more in redistributive than distributive terms, but this change in perceptions has begun only recently.

Political structures related to aging policy have developed parallel to this legislative pattern. Just as constituent politics for the aging or other groups yields categorically based constituent programs, so does it produce agencies and committees with clear constituent identifications. In aging, the familiar listing consists of: the agencies and councils on aging that now exist at all levels of government, special legislative committees, and task forces and other ad hoc bodies set forth around aging issues. The insistent desire—and the frequent formal recognition of that desire—for these bodies to be highly visible and autonomous has made for the creation of relatively discrete policy domains. Most recently this had led to the establishment of cabinet level departments on aging in many of the states. These moves have often been resisted by human service officials concerned with maintaining more encompassing administrative structures, but the trend in aging has been toward separate and visible structures.

Finally, aging policy has been *additive*. Earlier enactments provide a base from which subsequent actions can be launched; advocacy does not have to start from neutral or unoccupied territory. Medicare would not have come—at least not in 1965 —if there had not been Social Security on which to attach it; SSI would still be "OAA/AB/APTD" had not the Family Assistance Plan debate created an atmosphere making some kind of guaranteed income plan possible. More mundane but no less important is the implementation of a piece of legislation often providing the impetus for its own subsequent expansion. Whatever ideological hurdles had to be overcome during the original debate are since past, and work under the legislation creates a constituency whose natural concern is furtherance of that which put them in business. In aging, the existing policy base has allowed for the massive growth in spending which is the cause of so much current discussion. No major new spending legislation for the aging has been enacted since SSI, yet spending on behalf of older persons has more than doubled since that time. Clearly, the income and health care entitlement programs are responsible for virtually all of this growth, but it was existing legislation, demography, inflation, and political posturing that had more to do with this enormous increase than insistent pressure on a neutral or hostile environment.

The purpose of the above discussion, however brief, has been to indicate the constellation of contextual and proximate factors which have contributed to the policy gains that have benefitted the overall aging population to the present time. The presence of a large and growing aging population and groups organized on their behalf have played a role in many of the legislative enactments, but demands and pressures alone cannot account for the gains which have been made. Attitudes toward the aging, decision-makers' perceptions of the needs and utility of the aging, creation of official bodies identified with the aging and those serving them, and the cumulation of a corpus of policies assisting the aging have each worked to the advantage of the old age policy constituency.

THE CHANGING ENVIRONMENT AND RESEARCH

The major point to be raised concerning this set of policy relevant factors is that a number of contemporary trends point to a lessening of past sources of political support. Should this be the case, the aging are going to find their relatively favorable policy status in serious jeopardy. Prevailing attitudes, decision-makers' agendas, and the decision-making environment may, in particular, undergo significant transformations. In turn, this may mean that the future of old age policy will rest on the ingredients and dispositions posited by the demand/pressure model.

The reasons for the expected diminution in these past sources of support are becoming increasingly familiar to persons in the aging field. Regarding the longstanding supportive attitudes of the public to the needs of the aging, one now looks to the current antigovernmental spending mood and the data reviewed briefly earlier which suggest that the overall aging population is not so singularly disadvantaged as has historically been the case. While some studies continue to show a greater disposition toward supporting the aging than other social welfare constituencies, pervasive pressures to limit governmental spending cannot but limit the explosive rate of public spending for the aging as well as for other groups.

At the point where these pressures impinge on old age expenditures, the question then becomes where and how the limitations or cuts should be distributed. Middle and upper income groups will challenge any proposed major downward shifts in the OASI benefit formula, and current official thinking does not appear to be pointed in that direction. The short-run method for slowing growth in Medicare funding will be in increasing the deductible charge for hospital care and continuing to limit the amounts Medicare will pay for medical services rendered. Because these deductibles and reimbursable fees are not adjusted for income (unless the individual is Medicaid eligible), they place a heavy burden on the low income elderly. Medicaid targets its resources on low income persons—40% of expenditures going toward the low income elderly—but the program imposes a considerable state matching requirement, and Medicaid has become the largest single budgetary outlay in many of the states. With the antispending sentiment currently being directed heavily at state budgets, this is an item where pressure will be intense. Without an increase in the federal government's matching share for Medicaid services, the overall service money available on a per capita basis for the indigent elderly may decline. Social service funding—principally under the Older Americans Act and Title XX of the Social Security Act—is falling victim to inflation after dramatic increases in the early 1970s. Even at their expanded levels, these programs are far from meeting all legitimate need, with only 2% of persons eligible under the nutrition program, for example, actually receiving services. To this point, public sentiment has provided at least a "permissive consensus" for old age programs to grow, but cost pressures and the view that the elderly have received their fair share—whether warranted or not—are likely to yield a decline in this consensus.

These same pressures will impinge on governmental decision-makers. David Broder's (1978) appraisal that Congress from now on will be looking nervously over its shoulder when liberalization of Social Security benefits is on the agenda may apply to other programs as well. The needs are still there, as most will recognize, but the political advantages to be gained by addressing those needs with significant increases and redirection of funding may not be. Cutbacks for popular and constituency-based programs such as CETA and maternal health care are being proposed, and pressures, if not cutbacks, on aging programs cannot be far behind. There is no question that legislators will continue to speak and probably act on behalf of "the elderly" and their needs; but, the real question is how much of this will be, to repeat Mayhew's terms, advertising and credit-claiming and how much will involve coming up with funds to meet a broad spectrum of pressing needs.

It is here that demands and pressures from the aging and their advocates will take on a greater relative importance. The wide range of social welfare spending interests will be fighting a battle to restrict cuts on overall spending in that broad area. Within that loose coalition, aging interests will need to be active in protecting their relative position, while not letting differences among them weaken their overall position. In keeping with the tenets of the demand/pressure model, the aging and their organizations may find that they will be called on to employ the principal sanction they potentially have— withdrawal of electoral and organizational support for elected and other governmental officials. Whether they are capable of doing this on a collective basis remains very much open to question, but the evolving situation may, at least, provide a setting in which a fair test can be made.

As a last consideration here, fiscal and other constraints will bring added pressures to the agencies and organizations that currently constitute the aging policy arena. New policy initiatives are likely to be more focused, thereby reducing the discretion and latitude which both public and private aging organizations have enjoyed. Disbursement programs may find themselves confronted with regulatory requirements which had not encumbered them previously. Senior level governmental officials who were formerly uninvolved in aging policy matters are already making demands. Actors in other fields are likely to raise objections to new departures or expenditures in aging when they see such developments coming at their expense. Finally, new performance demands and concerns with accountability will confront the range of persons working in the aging field.

In all of this will be changes affecting the research community. Recent trends toward directed rather than investigator-initiated research will probably accelerate as officials increasingly demand program-specific information. The research constituency in aging will also find that its traditional sources of support will be opened to researchers identified with more generic problems in the social services, health care, and other areas where research has been aging-oriented and largely age-segregated. All of this may lead to a greater volume and diversity of research related to problems of the aging, but it will surely be unsettling to those who have had relatively singular access to particular sources of research funding. In research, as in the larger program areas with which research is associated, outside interest and imposition of outside agendas will be on the increase.

In concluding, it can only be emphasized once again that longstanding relations and patterns of activity in aging will be subjected to a range of new environmental stimuli. Such a change is unavoidable given the challenges and problems brought on by an aging population and the attention which must be devoted to it. In the long-run, one must hope that this new interest will lead to informed and humane responses, but in the short-run it will change the assumptions and routines which politicians, professionals, and researchers have brought to the aging field.

REFERENCES

ALMOND, G. and S. VERBA (1963) The Civic Culture. Princeton: Princeton University Press.
ALTMEYER, A. (1968) The Formative Years of Social Security. Madison: University of Wisconsin Press.
BAUER, R., I. POOL and L. DEXTER (1963) American Business and Public Policy. New York: Atherton Press.
BENGTSON, V. and N. CUTLER (1976) "Generations and intergenerational relations," pp. 130-159 in R. Binstock and E. Shanas (eds.) The Handbook of Aging and the Social Sciences. New York: Van Nostrand Reinhold.

BINSTOCK, R. (1978) "Federal policy toward the aging—its inadequacies and its politics." National Journal 45: 1838-1845.
—— (1972) "Interest group liberalism and the politics of aging." Gerontologist 12: 265-280.
—— and M. LEVIN (1976) "The Political Dilemmas of Intervention Policies," in Binstock R. and Shanas, E. (eds.), The Handbook of Aging and the Social Sciences. New York: Van Nostrand Reinhold.
BRODER, D. (1978) "The end of an era of liberal legislation." Boston Globe.
BURKE, V. J. and V. BURKE (1974) Nixon's Good Deed. New York: Columbia University Press.
BUTLER, D., and D. STOKES (1971) Political Changes in Britain. New York: St. Martin's.
CALIFANO, J. (1978) "The aging of America: questions for the four-generation society." Annals 438: 96-107.
CAMPBELL, A. (1971) "Politics through the life-cycle." Gerontologist 11: 112-117.
—— P. CONVERSE, W. MILLER, and D. STOKES (1960) The American Voter. New York: John Wiley.
CLEMENTE, F. (1975) "Age and the perception of national priorities." Gerontologist 15: 61-63.
CUTLER, N. E. (1977) "Demographic, social-psychological, and political factors in the politics of aging: a foundation for research in 'political gerontology.'" American Political Science Review 71: 1011-1025.
—— (1969) "Generation, maturation, and party affiliation: a cohort analysis." Public Opinion Quarterly 33: 583-588.
—— and V. BENGTSON (1974) "Age and political alienation: maturation, generation, and period effects." Annals 415: 160-175.
DAHL, R. (1967) Pluralist Democracy in the United States. Chicago: Rand McNally.
DAVIDSON, R. (1977) "Breaking up those 'cozy triangles': an impossible dream?" in S. Welch and J. Peters (eds.) Legislative Reform and Public Policy. New York: Praeger.
DERTHICK, M. (1975) Uncontrollable Spending for Social Services Grants. Washington, DC: Brookings.
DOUGLASS, E., W. CLEVELAND, and G. MADDOX (1974) "Political attitudes, age, and aging: a cohort analysis of archival data." Journal of Gerontology 29: 666-675.
DYE, T. (1972) Understanding Public Policy. Englewood Cliffs, NJ: Prentice-Hall.
EDELMAN, M. (1960) "Symbols and political quiescence." American Political Science Review 53: 695-704.
ELAZAR, D. (1972) American Federalism: A View from the States. New York: Crowell.
—— and J. ZIKMUND [eds.] (1975) The Ecology of American Political Culture. New York: Crowell.
ESTES, C. (1974) "Community planning for the elderly: a study in goal displacement." Journal of Gerontology 29: 684-691.
ESTES, C. E. (1978) "Political gerontology." Society 15: 43-49.

FEDER, J. (1977) "Medicare implementation and the policy process." Journal of Health Politics, Policy and Law 2: 173-189.

FESLER, J. (1965) "Approaches to the understanding of decentralization." Journal of Politics 27: 536-566.

FONER, A. (1972) "The polity," pp. 115-159 in M. Riley, M. Johnson, and A. Foner, (eds.) Aging and Society: Vol. 3, A Sociology of Age Stratification. New York: Russell Sage.

GLENN, N. (1974) "Aging and conservatism." Annals 415: 176-186.

——— (1969) "Aging, disengagement, and opinionation." Public Opinion Quarterly 33: 17-33.

——— and M. GRIMES (1968) "Aging, voting, and political interest." American Sociological Review 33: 563-575.

GLENN, N. and T. HEFNER (1972) "Further evidence on aging and party identification." Public Opinion Quarterly 36: 31-47.

HECLO, H. (1974) Modern Social Politics in Britain and Sweden. New Haven, CT: Yale University Press.

HOLTZMAN, A. (1963) The Townsend Movement: A Political Study. New York: Bookman.

HUDSON, R. (1978a) "The 'graying' of the federal budget and its consequences for old-age policy." Gerontologist 18: 428-440.

——— (1978b) "Review of The Gray Lobby." American Political Science Review 72: 1429-1430.

——— (1974) "Rational planning and organizational imperatives: prospects for area planning in aging." Annals 415: 41-54.

HUNT, C. (1960) "Private integrated housing in a medium size northern city." Social Problems 7: 196-209.

IGLEHART, J. (1978) "The cost of keeping the elderly well." National Journal 43: 1728-1731.

JENNINGS, M. K. and R. NIEMI (1975) "Continuity and change in political orientations: a longitudinal study of two generations." American Political Science Review 69: 1316-1335.

KILLIAN, L. and J. HAER (1958) "Variables related to attitudes regarding school desegregation among white southerners." Sociometry 21: 159-164.

KUHN, M. (1978) "Open letter." Gerontologist 18: 422-427.

LASSWELL, H. (1930) Psychopathology and Politics. Chicago: University of Chicago Press.

LINDBLOM, C. (1959) "The science of 'muddling through'." Public Administration Review 19: 79-88.

LIPSET, S. M. (1960) Political Man: The Social Bases of Politics. Garden City, NJ: Doubleday.

LOWI, T. (1969) The End of Liberalism. Boston: Norton.

——— (1964) "American business, public policy, case-studies, and political theory." World Politics 16: 677-715.

McCONNELL, G. (1967) Private Power and American Democracy. New York: Knopf.

MADDOX, G. (1978) "Reply [to M. Kuhn]" Gerontologist 18: 422-427.

MARMOR, T. (1970) The Politics of Medicare. Chicago, Aldine.
MARVICK, D. [ed.] (1961) Political Decision-Makers: Recruitment and Performance. Glencoe, Free Press.
MAYHEW, D. (1974) Congress: The Electoral Connection. New Haven, CT: Yale University Press.
MINTZ, M. (1979) "Two groups for elderly may lose nonprofit postal status." Washington Post, 2 February.
MUNNELL, A. (1976) "The future of Social Security." New England Economic Review (July/August): 3-28.
MURPHY, J. (1971) "Title I of ESEA: the politics of implementing federal education reform." Harvard Educational Review 41: 35-63.
National Journal (1978) The Economics of Aging. Washington, DC.
NEUSTADT, R. (1960) Presidential Power. New York: John Wiley.
NIE, N., S. VERBA, and J. KIM (1974) "Political participation and the life-cycle." Comparative Politics 6: 319-340.
PINNER, F., P. JACOBS, and P. SELZNICK (1959) Old Age and Political Behavior. Berkeley: University of California Press.
PRATT, H. (1976) The Gray Lobby. Chicago: University of Chicago Press.
——— (1974) "Old age associations in national politics." Annals 415: 106-119.
PRESSMAN, J. and A. WILDAVSKY (1973) Implementation. Berkeley: University of California Press.
REDFORD, E. (1969) Democracy in the Administrative State. New York: Oxford University Press.
SALISBURY, R. (1968) "The analysis of public policy: a search for theories and roles," pp. 151-175 in A. Ranney (ed.) Political Science and Public Policy. Chicago: Markham.
SAMUELSON, R. (1978a) "Benefits for elderly squeeze U.S. budget." National Journal 7: 256-260.
——— (1978b) "Aging America: who will shoulder the growing burden?" National Journal (October): 1712-1717.
SCHATTSCHNEIDER, E. (1960) The Semisovereign People. New York: Holt, Rinehart & Winston.
SAPOLSKY, H. (1977) "America's socialized medicine: the allocation of resources within the veterans' health care system." Public Policy 25 (Summer).
SCHLESINGER, A., Jr. (1958) The Politics of Upheaval. Boston: Houghton Mifflin.
SCHREIBER, E. and L. MARSDEN (1972) "Age and opinions on a government program of medical aid." Journal of Gerontology 27: 95-101.
SCHULZ, J. (1976) "Income distribution and the aging," pp. 561-591 in R. Binstock and E. Shanas (eds.) The Handbook of Aging and the Social Sciences. New York: Van Nostrand Reinhold.
SEARING, D., G. WRIGHT, and G. RABINOWITZ (1976) "The primacy principle: political socialization and belief systems." British Journal of Political Science, 6: 83-113.
SEIDMAN, H. (1977) Politics, Position, and Power, 2nd ed. New York: Oxford University Press.

SHANAS, E. (1978) "New directions in health care for the elderly," pp. 1-9 in J. Brookbank (ed.) Improving the Quality of Health Care for the Elderly. Gainesville, FL: Center for Gerontological Studies and Programs, University of Florida.

TINGSTEN, H. (1937) Political Behavior: Studies in Election Statistics. London: P. S. King.

U.S. Bureau of the Census (1975) "Demographic aspects of aging and the older population in the United States." Current Population Reports (Special Studies. Series P-23, No. 59). Washington, DC: Government Printing Office.

——— (1977) "Characteristics of the population below the poverty level." Current Population Reports (Series P-60, No. 106). Washington, DC: Government Printing Office.

U.S. Congressional Budget Office (1977) Poverty Status of Families under Alternative Definitions of Income. Washington, DC: Government Printing Office.

U.S. House of Representatives, Select Committee on Aging (1977) Federal Responsibility to the Elderly. Washington, DC: Government Printing Office.

U.S. National Center for Health Statistics (1978) Vital and Health Statistics: Current Estimates from the Health Interview Survey [Series 10: #52 (1969); #95 (1974); #126 (1978)]. Washington, DC: Government Printing Office.

U.S. Office of Management and Budget (1979) The Budget of the United States Government: FY 1980. Washington, DC: Government Printing Office.

VERBA, S. and N. NIE (1972) Participation in America: Political Democracy and Social Equality. New York: Harper & Row.

VINYARD, D. (1978) "The rediscovery of the elderly." Society 15: 24-29.

WATTS, H. and F. SKIDMORE (1977) "An update of the poverty picture plus a new look at relative tax burdens." Focus 2: 5-7, 12.

WEAVER, J. (1976) "The elderly as a political community: the case of national health policy." Western Political Quarterly 29: 610-619.

WILDAVSKY, A. (1964) The Politics of the Budgetary Process. Boston: Little, Brown.

WILSON, J. (1973) Political Organizations. New York: Basic Books.

ZANDER, M. (1978) "Welfare Reform and the Urban Aged." Society 15: 59-66.

8

THE POLITICS OF AGING AND
AGING RESEARCH

Harry Posman

The sociology of knowledge addresses the question, among others, as to what types of issues are considered significant by the knowledge-building community. Now that we have moved from a period of relatively high public expenditures to one where "less is more," it may not be entirely coincidental that in the field of aging there is increasing attention to the emerging specialty of political gerontology. As fiscal constraints impact on public expenditures, questions emerge concerning the allocation and targeting of resources and the conditions which affect the political process by which such decisions are made.

With increasing interest in the politics of aging it is useful to assess the current status of research activities and to suggest promising directions for future efforts. Hudson, in this volume, has outlined four basic areas of concern, summarized major findings of past research, and identified issues which require additional research. He reviewed research concerning the political participation and cohesion of older persons, aging-based interest groups, policies affecting older persons, and the changing sources of political support for policies benefiting the elderly. And, knowing well that "less is a bore" in the research arena, he has developed a preliminary agenda as a guide for future research.

After reviewing findings concerning the extent to which variations in political orientations are attributable to age, largely based on national survey data, research is suggested on the participation of the aged in state and local politics. Current studies supported by the Administration on Aging examine the legislative process in 26 states and the political impact of the elderly at the local level in Florida, where the future may be now. Research on the effects of Proposition 13 on programs for the elderly need to be supplemented with research on the extent to which older persons support the trend toward lessened governmental activity while protecting spending programs for the aged.

Research on organized groups advancing the interests of the elderly will provide knowledge of stated objectives as well as the effects of less evident organizational objectives on these policy positions. Of critical concern will be the role of these organized groups when public policy shifts from a "body count" approach to a targeting of limited resources on the "vulnerable" elderly—those who are very old, functionally impaired and socially isolated. Representing the majority of relatively well elderly, the present orientations of the aging-oriented organizations are defined in part by their membership bases. A significant policy initiative toward the concentration of resources in behalf of a relatively small, disadvantaged segment of the older population will have major implications for these organizations. In addition, at the local level, organized efforts may be emerging which articulate the interests of disadvantaged minorities outside the established organizations of older persons. Research is needed to examine the natural history of such local advocacy groups, the extent to which they succeed in advancing the interests of their constituencies, and their organizational viability.

A major part of the research resources of the Administration on Aging is allocated to the study of current and alternate policies which affect older persons in such areas as income, employment, retirement, continued opportunities for work, education and leisure, housing and living arrangements, and health care and services. Their objective is to identify the consequences of current policies for the elderly and suggest modifications which will enhance the well-being of older persons. The triad of concerns—need, equity, and cost—are reflected in research priorities which focus on low-income, minority, rural, and underserved older persons. Current research examines efforts to expand the allocation of existing resources on behalf of the elderly (e.g., Title XX), the needs of different subpopulations, the extent to which minority and rural elderly have equal access to public benefits and services, and the cost-effectiveness of different intervention modalities. The concern for the vulnerable elderly is reflected in the support of policy studies concerning intervention strategies and delivery mechanisms in the area of community-based service systems.

Indications of a lessening of past sources of political support for legislative enactments on behalf of older persons have been noted. As resources stabilize, increased effort is directed to maintaining existing allocations, targeting of programs, and increasing the performance of support systems. Research is required to meet the information needs of public officials at all levels of government who are concerned with these issues. To the extent that the knowledge-building community is sensitive to current trends and conditions, research will be focused on issues which are seen as significant and relevant by managers, planners, and practitioners concerned with programs for the elderly.

SECTION

V

CONCLUSION

9

VALUES AND FUTURE NEEDS
FOR RESEARCH

Martin B. Loeb and Edgar F. Borgatta

There are several obvious caveats about future needs for research. First, the federal government, particularly through the Administration on Aging and the National Institute on Aging, will let us know what research will be needed. This is a factual statement and not a matter of cynicism. Many gerontolgists and other scientists will consult on what is important, but the provision of money for the research will effectively demonstrate that a "need" for the research exists.

A second point is that research will go on by many of the same people who have done it in the past, and they will do the same kinds of research with elaborations and extensions. In other words, the future research in aging will be more of what we have been doing because we do not know how to do much different. Again, that is not meant to be a negative statement but a statement of fact. Thus, we will see continued biological research about aging. Demographers will keep busy cutting up the population by age, sex, race, residence, and so forth; they will elaborate their projections. There will be more and more research that is essentially descriptive economics—the details of the economic wellbeing of the elderly. And there will be a variety of social psychological research that deals with friendship patterns, intergenerational studies, studies of kinship systems, and so on. There will be continuing research on degenerative diseases.

There has been a long investment of very good research on all diseases, and there has been an increase in expected length of life. But to anybody who studies this research on disease, it appears that very little more is expected which will essentially increase the expected length of life. In other words, we may not be far from a point where instead of dying from a disease, on some given day, based on our genes, we would fall over dead. This may be a little extreme, but diseases are being controlled, and it is quite evident that the proportion of persons living beyond 75 years is still increasing. If disease is taken care of, then what does one die of?

If people will be around longer and become more frail, essentially people will not only become "old-old," but very old-old; research is needed on how to make life more comfortable for them. What makes life more pleasant? How is life enhanced? What will be needed is research on caring rather than research on curing. Since there have been problems and disease, our culture has pushed for annihilation of peoples' troubles: to do away with diseases, with poverty, with bad housing—to provide cures. Our service system is not tuned properly because our value system has not yet moved to the idea of reducing discomfort. As a matter of fact, within our value heritage there is still some strength to the notion that one should learn to live with discomfort and adversity. It is good for the soul and character. Most readers will be familiar with the hospice movement. Some consider it a revolutionary kind of activity. Some may be shocked about hospices when they understand what they do. What they do is make people as comfortable as possible during their dying weeks. The people that developed this approach have used all sorts of techniques that go directly against all "good practice." For example, addictive drugs are made available. In England, heroin is available. In the United States, a doctor might say: "I wouldn't use those drugs, they are addictive." It is an attitude; it is a part of a value system. Most things done in community care, health care, and so on, are approaches to curing rather than caring. If one considers mental health clinics, if one works with children who are presumed to have a whole lifetime ahead of them, then an emphasis on curing makes sense. But for elderly people with some dementias, not much is going to be done with regard to curing. Interventions may not make much difference in a cure, but they can be diverted to other proposals. If practitioners see their job as mobilizing resources to make life pleasant rather than to cure, then they can be successful. A reasonable projection is that there will be more research about interventions that make people comfortable.

A second area that will need research is the whole delivery system problem. There is a value in our culture that independent living is better than dependent living. There is no evidence that people are better off in their own homes than they are in a good communal circumstance. For example, there are some good nursing homes. It is not clear whether it is better to be an isolate in one's own home or to have access to some group activity.

If one looks at nursing home economics (or other group quarters), it is evident that most of their capital maintenance costs go for expensive life safety protections (sprinkler systems, fire doors, and the like). In times of limited resources, a few lives may be saved every year at the expense of not providing more social, psychological, and other comforts to people in group quarters. It is easy to have laws which deal with rules governing safety devices. People can check how wide the door is, how thick it is, what it is made of, how far apart the sprinklers are, and so forth. What is difficult is to find people who can help these nursing homes and group quarters to provide a life enhancing quality rather than a life saving one.

Some research will be needed on what actually disturbs the elderly. The old-old have a problem in addition to their illness: they lose many of their close friends and intimates. It is not clear that we understand how the old feel about these experiences. If they suffer, how can we provide ways of dealing with grief and loss? They not only lose them by death. (Death is one thing that has given old age a bad name.) Pretty nearly all dying is now done by the elderly—a very recent change. But that is not the only thing that separates the elderly from their friends and family. People are mobile and people change their occupation and status. One of the changes that takes place is retirement.

Some values, such as the way retirement is received, need to be studied. For example, it has been noted that, contrary to many expectations, retirement is not received negatively by most. Many, if not most, look forward to it. In Scandinavia, retirement is not stigmatized; neither is unemployment—they enjoy it. That is because they do not have much of it, and they organize to deal with the event systematically. But one of the characteristics about being able to deal with role changes is being able to practice. In Sweden, the law requires everybody to take fairly long vacations every year. So, one begins early in life to develop alternate life styles. For the old age of our children, we may need to do some research now, helping them socialize to whatever adaptations they will have to make in old age. One can wonder whether the existentialism of some of the young is going to stand them in good stead in their old age. Those who are work oriented may be the ones that feel retirement deprives them of, rather than provides them with, opportunity. Retirement may or may not be difficult for most people. At least it is not traumatic; but it is difficult if one has to change very many things in one's life. So, research must be addressed to what it is that happens early in life that will enhance life in later years.

VALUES AND THE AGING POPULATION

The values implicit in viewing the aging process are often competitive. In American society a great deal of value is placed on the potential productive contribution of each individual—economically and otherwise. The society is also oriented toward mobility, and mobility depends either on expansion to provide opportunities or retirement of individuals in the system so that they may be replaced. Thus, on the one hand there may be encouragement and inducement to keep older persons working; and, on the other hand, there may be pressure for them to retire.

There are possible conflicts that may arise in values from the point of view of the older person. For example, individuals may view their life as one in which they work, earn, and accumulate, and then, reaching mature ages, they feel entitled to rest, peace, and security, and presumably to the pleasures and privileges of leisure that they have foregone. There is a strong emphasis on work as a means of satisfying one's own creative desires, of expressing oneself, and of getting satisfaction from the work itself and also from colleagues and coworkers. Since a substantial potential for very many satisfactions is associated with work, people may hesitate and postpone retiring.

From the point of view of families that are in the life cycle, those in earlier periods are likely not to be concerned particularly with the problems of the aged except as they experience the problems through their parents and relatives. But, with a detachment that is as old as civilization, one does not generalize too efficiently to one's own potential experience, and sympathy with the problems of the aged may not be as strong and direct as is appropriate when one takes into account just how inevitable old age is. From this point of view, it may be seen that the values of the society may create a push from below to move older persons out of the productive system to make room for those coming up. At the same time, because of seniority systems, older persons may also be more rewarded (higher values). Thus, for example, in many professions, older persons are more expensive for the operation of the system, and it is not necessary that the higher cost of maintaining the older worker leads to better products. Indeed, in some areas there is an expected reduction in the efficiency of older workers, so the incongruity develops that older workers may be paid higher wages for less productivity. Again, this would introduce concern in terms of institutional forces for the retirement of such workers.

It should be noted that the above statements are suggestions and not facts. They suggest the kinds of values that individuals may have and that may be common in the social system; they do not raise issues as to what the facts actually are.

Part of the concern associated with problems of aging is attributed to the increase in age of persons in the sense of extension of average length of life. Progressively, the potential for living to the ages of 70, 80, and 90, has increased as medicine (and other facilities) has improved. However, if this were a simple slow progression, simple slow solutions could be applied.

One of the factors that make aging such an explosive problem for society is the dislocation associated with the irregularities of the fertility rates in society. Historically, we are looking forward to a situation in which relatively small numbers born during the Depression will be entering the ranks of the aged. These modest cohorts have been supporting somewhat larger groups from earlier, more fertile periods, but the rates of support—the actual expectations of what one may expect from the system with regard to minimum standards of living—have been increasing. Also, already the larger cohorts from the post-World War II period in the labor force contribute heavily to the tax base and resources used in the Social Security system. The group in the post-World War II baby boom becomes an enormous support base for the Social Security system and other programs serviced by current tax contributions rather than equity accumulations as is common in private pension funds.

The type of concern that develops—and thus accentuates concern with aging and the aged with regard to the future—is that after the long period of high fertility following the post World War II, the fertility rates have dropped markedly to the levels of low fertility during the Depression. There is a mass of persons who are traveling in these cohorts from the post-World War II baby boom that will eventually arrive at the retirement ages. On the basis of current expectations, those who will be there to earn income and support the retirees through Social Security will be numerically diminished. The ratio of retirees and the aged to productive workers could increase sharply, and unless there is continued expansion of the economy at a high rate of efficiency on a per worker basis, the potential burden on the younger group will be enormous. This, then, is the global spectre with which we live. It is not merely a matter of having an aging population having an extended length of life; the irregularities historically present are the more visible and acute threat.

Aside from the threat of having to support an increasing aged population that may be rampant in the thoughts of our youth, other dislocations are created by the uneven fertility rates that have existed historically. For example, we had a tremendous growth in education during the baby boom, and as the baby boom has aged, the demand for teachers and professors has been shrinking. First, elementary and high school teachers were surplus and then college professors. Concern has shifted in the direction of raising the issue of whether people should continue to be trained for surplus occupations, potentially reducing further the demand for education. Similarly, industries oriented around young people flourished as the baby boom provided larger markets; but, subsequently, demand has attenuated. Presumably, some stability in birth rates could be projected, but there is no way of knowing that another baby boom could not develop. The culture has been changing quickly with regard to expectations around sex roles, but since these attitudes may be subject to a swing back, it simply is not possible to predict what will occur. What is clear is that, at the current stage of dislocation because of the uneven fertility performance over the last decades, we face some serious problems. All these problems, related to aspects of the population in characteristics, essentially are topics for future research.

SOCIAL SECURITY COSTS AND VALUE SYSTEMS

One area that will require considerable research may be strictly economic, but has major implications relative to the orientations to government that become the way of life. In particular, the idea of Social Security, which was so acceptable as a small tax with great benefits, has come to face the realities of the real costs involved and whether or not the program is insurance or welfare.

The Social Security taxes currently constitute approximately 40% of the taxes collected by the federal government. Under the circumstances, it becomes difficult to think of this collection as a matter of *insurance* payments, and indeed, very few people deny the notion of *tax* as in "payroll tax." There is, however, a residue of a notion of insurance. This is manifest in a number of ways. For example, benefit eligibility is related to length of participation. And, benefits are related to payments into the system. These relations, however, merely suggest the parallelism to insurance programs, and are no way definitional. Recent history has raised the level of concern with the ability of Social Security to maintain its viability, since at one point the system was "headed for bankruptcy" unless tax rates or wage bases were increased. The magnitude of involvement in everyday life can be noted by the fact that, currently, the tax rate for Social Security is 12.26%, 6.13% of which is paid by the individual from his taxable wage base and 6.13% of which is paid by the employer for the individual. The wage base is $22,900, and the taxes for 1979 are $2,806.

The estimate is that the maximum tax will have doubled from 1979 to 1986. Some questions of appropriate research in these areas require going beyond the economic analyses and asking questions of what implications in the implementation of current policy are for governmental style and ultimately for other aspects of social governments. It must be remembered that the current system and alternatives are not the only ones available, although it always becomes difficult to alter policies once they are instituted and, particularly, once vested interest groups become beneficiaries of policies. For example, what are the value systems that people hold, whether they are the common voters or nonvoters of the society, the social reformers, or the politically central elites? Where will the system take us in terms of form of government, and where presumably, do people wish to go? For example, if the first notions associated with Social Security were to provide minimum benefits at a time when none existed for the masses in American society, how far beyond providing a minimum is the system to go? Similarly, if the idea was one of providing a minimum for all individuals eventually, then is this necessarily tied to a notion of insurance which returns benefits in proportion to payments made? It is conceivable, for example, that an alternate system at this time could be viable in which the so called welfare aspects could be encompassed by one form of taxation, and *insurance benefits could be separated from these.*

The concept of minimum benefits that could be separated from a notion of annuity purchase and insurance does not leave an unambiguous notion of implicit values. In particular, it may be thought of as welfare in the usual sense of providing for those who are not able to provide for themselves, or it may be thought of as providing a minimum, which would be the baseline from which all persons operate. These are values that are not coextensive, and about which relatively little is known in terms of the operation of government in general. The issues

have become visible in other arenas where government subsidies are provided and support systems have been developed,
but clarification of the issues involved in the value systems
implicit and their consequences for the future form of government still have to be explored.

One aspect of this problem constantly arises as the notion
that the "middle class" is being penalized by being squeezed
from two sides. It is presumably pushed to achieve, and then it
is penalized for achieving. The issue comes up in a second way
with regard to the provision of resources for the poor for which
"means tests" are used. Thus, for example, if a means test is
gauged at a particular dollar value, often the availability of
benefits are on a basis of all or none. More to the point, there
are often many benefits which become available on the basis of
means tests, so that individuals may be borderline to the
benefits, and because they are borderline they may be excluded
from the majority of benefits; whereas, having just slightly
less income, they could have access to a number of benefits.
There is obviously awkwardness in this type of structure, but it
is one that has been commonplace and ingrained in the system
to a point that very often there is an unwillingness to explore
alternatives to such a system. Alternatives to the common
means test have been advanced, and one rather radical but
interesting proposal suggests that *benefits that are universally
available should be universally distributed.* Thus, for example,
if a minimum standard of money income is visualized as necessary for all persons, then presumably one option would be to
have the transfer system provide every individual *directly* with
that minimum. That minimum, presumably, would be not subject to tax. However, all other income would be subject to tax,
much as taxes are collected today. But, presumably, the tax
system would then need to be adjusted to increase the monies
needed for the initial transfer. Such a proposal sounds much
more radical than it actually is, since, for example, at this
point, only a very small percentage of the population of the
United States is below the poverty level when income in both

money and services are considered. The transfer system, thus, would really not need to account for a great deal of additional real money.

Such proposals, of course, tend to be more radical in other ways. For example, the notion that people should be given the income which is considered to be sufficient for them to live minimally, rather than to have big brother watch and hand out the resources, may not be something that some people find attractive. Similarly, such suggestions very often are presumed to remove the need for various types of programs, and from the point of view of the system as a whole, such an orientation could cause a great deal of unemployment by the reduction of government bureaucracies.

What has been alluded to is the fact that there are basic values that are involved in how public policy is manifest. And we have been in a period of relatively rapid change and growth of government in recent decades. Experiments that have been carried out in other western or more modern industrialized states sometimes appear to provide models from which one can learn, but in other occasions leave as many or more questions unanswered.

Still, with the growing proportions of the aged, who are supposed to increase to roughly 12 to 14% of the population, the reality of a major segment of the population involved in a universal support system monitored through the government raises many issues of values that require exploration and detailed attention. This should focus not merely on the values of the legislators, nor of the so called educated professional, but should deal with concepts of equity and distributive justice at levels that range from the wishes of the common people to an examination of philosophical systems which may be competitive.

MANDATING LIFESTYLES

A major problem in discussing value systems that may be potential alternatives to the one which has evolved is that only after experience is accumulated can the consequences of given policies be assessed. The idea that there are unintended consequences to actions is as old as recorded history, but in the complex society in which planning has ostensibly become a key word, obtaining a perspective is often extremely difficult.

The phenomenon of fads also is ancient, but because the communication and transportation systems are quite different from what they were, and a greater segment of the population can be involved in various types of societal activities, fads and movements can sweep broadly and pervasively into the lifestyles of a nation. There can be student movements, Beatles, beef strikes, and the like. Sometimes things begin with strong positive values, great support, and then end as something different. The open enthusiasm for students becoming concerned can shift to concern with students because they are involved in other than academic endeavors and may be interfering with other societal processes. Concern with the environment may shift from protecting the resources to an alternate form of analysis which suggests that those that *have* are trying to keep those who *have not* from gaining access to natural resources. Definitions change as these developments proceed in history.

With regard to older persons, a number of these orientations have undergone change, and only in time can these be evaluated properly. Thus, for example, a policy in the Social Security system designed to keep persons who are 65 and older from working by penalizing $1.00 for every $2.00 earned above the given base may be laudable because it encourages people to retire. Still, this may be seen more and more as the imposition of a lifestyle. If the policy is removed and those 65 and older are not penalized for earnings, it may turn out that very little behavior actually changes, and most persons will indeed not remain in the labor market. Such questions should be examined. But in lifestyle, why should not those few who wish to work be permitted to do so? In such matters the potential for research continues and involves much more than dealing with the economics of support systems. What becomes involved in such questions is the study of behavior and of the dispositions of older persons.

But, in addition, the values involved in the initial policy may come under question and be phrased in a context other than the initial intentions of the proposers of the policy. So, among other things, many of the policies, which are designed to assist particular groups, or to protect some groups may turn out to have the strange, but real personification of that diffusely attributed generalization: "No good deed goes unpunished." If a person participates in a productive way in society, he may be penalized. If a person saves, it may be that he is penalized. If a person works harder, he may be penalized. So often, in our bureaucratic traces, this leveling philosophy seems to prevail. The homely old virtues frequently become ugly and undesirable in bureaucratic solutions to problems (effort, talent, success, sacrifice, deferring of gratifications, devotion to duty or others, and so on), and end up being penalties. It would be of some interest if studies, which dealt with the consequences of policies, focused on the values and the lifestyles mandated by these policies.

RECOGNITION OF AGE LIMITATIONS AND AGE DISCRIMINATION IN SOCIETY

There are physiological changes that occur with age; one has merely to look at the younger ages and observe the process of maturation. But how these changes proceed in later life and what they mean is something that is left relatively ambiguous. There are known major changes in later life, such as menopause, the reduction in taste buds, speed in healing, and so forth, but individuals vary sufficiently so that generalizations are difficult to make with regard to the age cycle. Still, within certain bounds, certain forms of limitations arise with age that can be noted as relatively incontravertible. Thus, for example, assuming random selection and sample size large enough, it is known that 25-year-olds will be active for five years longer than 30-year-olds. If in no other way, age serves as this type of limitation. Thus, some ground for limitations by age needs to be granted.

Still, how important these limitations should be viewed and when and how they should be utilized to limit persons is an area that still needs considerable study. Thus, for example, the United States Commission on Civil Rights has found that some schools, but particularly medical schools, discriminate against older persons in admission solely on the basis of age. From the point of view of medical schools, the schools can be more productive if they have students who will practice their professions longer. These facts of age will not be argued here; but assuming tasks with the benefit of additional experience and maturity is sometimes a virtue. Obviously, such matters are not cut and dried, and so what is required is a study of values and possibly the analysis of alternatives that are permissive, making it possible (even though unlikely and difficult) for persons who are still active but quite a bit older to initiate new careers even when it requires long preparation.

The limitations of age are, in the sense noted above, unavoidable. Other limitations that exist in society are sometimes mutable, and sometimes it is not known whether or not they can be changed. Thus, for example, differences in average length of life for different races is usually attributed to differences in life experiences, particularly those associated with socioeconomic standards. Differences between the sexes, on the other hand, is advanced as something which has greater basis in biology. Still, there are forceful arguments that the environments of males and females in the same society are different. Men have had different exposure occupationally, and, in addition, have been more associated with debilitating habits such as smoking and heavy drinking. Research will need to continue in the matter of sexual differences and the consequences of life style changes in the sexual roles of the average length of life. These studies have interesting potential since some changes that are noted in terms of equating opportunities and behavior are occurring in quite radical ways. It is noted, for example, that among teenagers, girls now smoke more than boys; what used to be seen as a masculine habit has now become feminine. With the highly touted consequences of smoking on health, possibly there will be an equation of average length of life on the sexes. On the other hand, fairly important changes have occurred in what is smoked, so it is not clear whether it is more likely that women will be dying earlier or that men will be living longer, if indeed the smoking habit is all that important.

Two reasons that the comments on sex differences in average length of life are important are as follows. First, if it is confirmed that the differences between the sexes are biologically based and virtually immutable, then the rational for giving recognition to such differences has to be explored further. (For example, will there be a prohibition against using male and female life tables in retirement annuity computations for retirement? If such a prohibition were to occur, logic would also require that the differences between 65-year-olds and 69-year-olds be ignored, since the difference of four years is the current best estimate of difference in expected average length of life at age 65 for the two sexes.) Second, if the differences are not biological, then more research should go into those factors that are associated with average length of life in order to increase awareness of how sex role differences affect health and length of life. While there is considerable examination of the causes of illness and problems of health, attention to the sexual differences on such matters is not explicit enough.

CHANGING NEEDS WITH REGARD TO RETIREMENT BENEFITS

Some of the issues that have arisen because of challenges to existing concepts of equality of treatment for men and women have reminded observers of the historically changing values. Thus, for example, Social Security occurred because people were not providing for themselves. It was advanced for this purpose, but as noted elsewhere, the confusion of whether it was insurance or welfare did not become problematic until recently. Similarly, motivation for the development of annuity insurance (TIAA) for teachers revolved around the notion that too many teachers were retiring without resources for self support. TIAA is private insurance, and the origins are in the philanthropic concerns of a private foundation. The development, however, ultimately was of an insurance form, but the regulations and agreements governing the insurance are designed to protect the participants against themselves. This made sense when the programs began, but now that Social Security and other federal programs provide the *minimum* needs for a retiree, there is some question about how they should be administered.

Indeed, changes in the system are admissible and available potentially, but the philosophy has not yet caught up with the possible challenges that may be raised on the basis of values. For example, the benefits provided under TIAA most commonly are on the basis of the purchase of annuities of equal value to the amount paid in by males or females, and the annuities commonly are based on separate life tables for each. The notion here is not pure, but initially the concept is that equal amounts are contributed by employers for the purchase of annuities on the grounds that there should be equal pay for equal work for the sexes. If different life tables are used for males and females, to provide equal *monthly* payments, employers would have to require a greater contribution from female employees, or both. The problems associated with the precedent that exists and the challenge which suggests that there should be movement in the direction of equal monthly payments could easily be by-passed by making more alternatives available to the employees on retirement. However, in terms of values involved, *this would require removal of the concept that the employee should be protected against him or herself.* So, for example, additional alternatives which would remove all the current problems could include the following: 1) Allow the retiree to withdraw the funds in his annuity account by a schedule entirely of the retiree's design, including the option of 100% withdrawal; 2) Make one of the options a nondiminishing payment schedule, based on current earnings of the entire annuity account, permitting the retiree to pass the total value of the accumulated funds into his or her estate when deceased.

The first alternative suggests that individuals should be given the option of doing what they want with monies that presumably are their own. Thus if a person wishes, he or she could put it into a conservative bond fund with a high yield, but allowing maintenance of the principal which could be redistributed subsequently. Or the retiree could simply take the funds and live it up for as long as the funds lasted, and then the retiree could live at the minimum subsistence levels available through Social Security or other resources. The second alternative still implies that the retirees must be protected against themselves but at least allows the option of controlling the ultimate disposal of the principal. Both of these procedures make the question of life tables irrelevant.

Partial alternatives of this type already exist. For example, the TIAA allows drawing of 10% of the annuity value on retirement as an adjustment resource. Similarly, many other retirement systems allow a person to withdraw all the funds that are tax exempt (on which taxes have already been paid), in general the contribution of the employee to the fund. The point is that the two suggestions above are extensions rather than radical departures and reflect some of the value changes that may be occurring.

By contrast, apparently without polling the membership about values or historical perspectives, the American Association of University Professors and the Association of American Colleges recently reissued "Principles on Academic Retirement and Insurance Plans" in which the same notion that funds should be returned to participants *only* in the form of an annuity was unchanged. Research in changing values in this area are needed but also in the presumed consequences of change. Are people really going to squander their money if they are given control of it in later life? This stereotype of incompetence seems inappropriate.

In this area of values around retirement funds, much additional research can be suggested. For example, the methods of vesting retirement funds imply that the worker is not due them until a sufficient period of time has been spent with a company or union, and specific ways of vesting often provide rigid demands on the participants. To whom are such procedures of advantage? The Company? The Union? The Participant? Such matters have frequently been managed by bargaining and politicing at the organizational level, and the issues of individual control have been ignored. Other systems of mobility of persons exist without penalizing the participants, so that such issues may be appropriate for study for the clarification of the values involved and raising objective questions of who such systems in fact, serve.

CONCLUDING COMMENT

We have noted some imminent matters that will need research in the future, but the emphasis has been largely to point out how values are intimately tied to both what we call change and what we expect currently and in the future. The values of the society are not clearly defined and singular, and so policies by the government often are stated in generalities that have to be interpreted by bureaucracies. The whole process requires study, and, more specifically, the actual values that come into play in the implementation of policies now requires study. What is required is not only the study of the needs of the aged, of the population in general, or the current status of the aged, but of what the values are that are currently determining policy and the values that are being determined by policy. The future of society is too important to be left to the haphazard bureaucratic processes which now appear to be operating.

ABOUT THE AUTHORS

EDGAR F. BORGATTA is the Research Director of the CASE Center for Gerontological Studies and Professor in the graduate faculty of sociology and of social psychology and personality. Formerly Brittingham Research Professor at the University of Wisconsin-Madison, Dr. Borgatta has written extensively on sociological methods and statistics, and is the President of the Research Committee on Logic and Methodology for the International Sociological Association. He has also been a faculty member at Harvard, Cornell and New York Universities, Dr. Borgatta is coeditor of *Research on Aging: A Quarterly of Social Gerontology.*

MARJORIE H. CANTOR holds the chair of Brookdale Professor of Gerontology at Fordham University's Graduate School of Social Services. Professor Cantor is also the Director of Research with Fordham's All-University center on Gerontology. For nine years prior to coming to Fordham she served as Director of the Office of Research for the New York City Department of Aging. In that capacity she was principal investigator for the following research: "The Elderly in the Inner City;" "Re-Entering the Work Force in the Later Years;" and "The Mentally Frail Elderly." Professor Cantor is the author of *The Health Crisis of Older People.*

DONNA COHEN is an Assistant Professor in the Department of Psychology and Behavioral Sciences and Head of the Geriatric Psychology Program at the University of Washington in Seattle. She was one of the planners of the 1971 White House Conference on Aging. Dr. Cohen chairs the Research Sub-Committee of the university's Institute on Aging, the Nursing Home Sub-Committee of the Long Term Comprehensive Care Committee, and the Joint Aging Seminars of the Department of Psychology and Behavioral Sciences.

CARL EISDORFER is Chairman of the Department of Psychiatry and Professor of Psychology at the University of Washington in Seattle. He is also Acting Director of the university's Institute on Aging. Dr. Eisdorfer was Director of Training and Research (1965-1970) and then Director (1970-1972) at the Duke University Center for the Study of Aging and Human Development. His recent interests involve the cognitive and emotional disturbances affecting the aged as well as the issues related to the psychiatric and psychopharmacological treatment of the aged. Professor Eisdorfer served as a principal consultant and was a frequent guest on Hugh Downes' TV show "Over Easy," the television program designed for senior citizens. Dr. Eisdorfer is Editor-in-Chief of the *Annual Review of Gerontology*.

RAYMOND HARRIS is Clinical Associate Professor of Medicine at Albany Medical College of Union University and President, Center for the Study of Aging, Albany. A prominent cardiologist and geriatrician, he maintains an active involvement in community issues involving the aged in the Albany area. Dr. Harris has written *Guide to Fitness After Fifty* and *The Management of Geriatric Cardiovascular Disease*. He is also on the editorial committee of the *Cardiac Rehabilitation Quarterly* and the *Journal of Gerontology*. His activities with the Gerontological Society have grown in depth and variety since 1960.

ROBERT B. HUDSON is Assistant Professor of Politics and Social Welfare in the Florence Heller Graduate School for Advanced Studies in Social Welfare at Brandeis University. He completed his doctoral studies in political science at the University of North Carolina in 1972. He is presently involved in a study of the "Critical Linkages in Health and Aging Policies" as part of a Research Career Development Award from the NIA/NIH. With Robert H. Binstock he contributed the article on "Political Systems and Aging" in

Binstock and Shanas (eds.), *The Handbook of Aging and the Social Sciences.*

EUGENE LITWAK is currently Professor of Sociology and Social Work at Columbia University where he also received his Ph.D. in the Department of Sociology in 1958. Dr. Litwak's interests include the complementary roles of primary groups and formal organizations in industrial society and the forms of linkage between them. He is conducting a research project on the structure of kinship, friendship, marriage, and the neighborhood in old age and the unique forms of aid provided by these groups to older persons.

MARTIN B. LOEB received his undergraduate training at the University of Toronto and took his doctorate at the University of Chicago. At Chicago he was a Fellow in the Department of Anthropology and a member of the Committee on Human Development. Professor Loeb has also taught in the School of Social Welfare of the University of California at Los Angeles. Since 1961 he has been on the faculty of the University of Wisconsin and in 1973 became Director of its Faye McBeath Institute on Aging and Adult Life. He was one of the founders of the Association for Gerontology in Higher Education, serving as president in 1974-1975. Dr. Loeb is co-editor of *Research on Aging: A Quarterly of Social Gerontology.*

NEIL G. McCLUSKEY is Director of the Center for Gerontological Studies, a unit within the Center for Advanced Study in Education (CASE) at the City University of New York Graduate School, an enterprise he helped bring into existence four years ago as chairman of a CUNY faculty planning group. A former student of Jean Piaget in Geneva, Professor McCluskey has combined the humanities and the social sciences in his teaching and scholarly career. Along with administrative responsibilities in the City University, the University of Notre Dame, and Gonzaga University, he has continued to publish and lecture extensively here and abroad. His research interests are in the area of life-quality for the aging, and life-transition planning. He is among the authors in the new Doubleday volume *The New Old: Struggling for Decent Aging* and the 1979 Wordsworth collection, *Gerontology in Higher Education: Developing Institutional and Community Strength.*

ABRAHAM MONK is Brookdale Professor of Gerontology in the School of Social Work of Columbia University. His prior teaching included positions at the State University of New York at Buffalo and the University of Buenos Aires. His research interests have focused on the analysis and evaluation of direct service systems to the aged. Professor Monk is presently Vice President of the Gerontological Society and Chairperson of the Social Research, Planning, and Practice Section of the Society. While lecturing in 1976 as Fulbright-Hays Senior Scholar at the University of Haifa he received the Max Prochovnick Memorial Award from the Israel Gerontological Society.

CHARLOTTE F. MULLER is Professor of Economics and Associate Director of the CUNY Graduate School's Center for Social Research. She has served as Acting Director of the CUNY Research Training Program in Urban Gerontology. Her interests in gerontology have brought her to a large-scale study on methods of physician reimbursement under Medicare. Her present work is financed through a contract with the Health Care Financing Administration of the Department of Health, Education and Welfare.

HARRY POSMAN is Director, Division of Research and Evaluation, Administration on Aging, Department of Health, Education and Welfare. Before serving in Washington he was a faculty member at Cornell University, the University of Connecticut, and the State University of New York at Albany. He has held positions in research and research management with federal, state, and voluntary agencies. One of his central interests is geriatric rehabilitation, an area in which he has done field experiments.